TALES FROM THE
DODGERS
DUGOUT

TALES FROM THE

DODGERS

DUGOUT

A COLLECTION OF THE GREATEST DODGER STORIES EVER TOLD

CARL ERSKINE

FOREWORD BY

VIN SCULLY

SPORTS
PUBLISHING

Sports Publishing books may be purchased in bulk at special discounts for sales promotion, corporate gifts, fund-raising, or educational purposes. Special editions can also be created to specifications. For details, contact the Special Sales Department, Sports Publishing, 307 West 36th Street, 11th Floor, New York, NY 10018 or sportspubbooks@skyhorsepublishing.com.

Sports Publishing® is a registered trademark of Skyhorse Publishing, Inc.®, a Delaware corporation.

Visit our website at www.sportspubbooks.com.

10 9 8 7 6 5 4 3 2

Library of Congress Cataloging-in-Publication Data is available on file.

Cover design by Tom Lau
Cover photo credit: AP Images

ISBN: 978-1-68358-026-3
Ebook ISBN: 978-1-68358-035-5

Printed in the United States of America

I dedicate this book to a range of people, all linked together over my lifetime. In the beginning was my Creator, who blessed me with some talents in baseball. Then my dad, Matt, and my brothers, Lloyd and Donald, who helped me develop them. Ray Brann, a good semipro player, who encouraged me. Archie Chadd and Charles Cummings, my high school coaches. About this time, my best girl, Betty Palmer, entered my life. She lived through every stage of my career with me while raising Danny, Gary, Susan, and Jimmy. They, too, shared some of the experiences.

Stanley Feezle, a Brooklyn Dodger scout who had just signed Gil Hodges, followed me in high school, along with my catching buddy, Jack Rector, and recommended us to the Dodgers.

Of course, Branch Rickey, who signed me in 1946 and was my mentor in baseball and a strong influence in my life. There are countless others in my hometown of Anderson, Indiana, who boosted and supported me.

I also dedicate this book to the baseball fans whose lives have been touched in some way by a pitch, a play, a game, or a season and who still write me about those wonderful years when I went to work every day at the ballpark and put on my No. 17 Dodger uniform.

Finally, I dedicate this book to The Game. Yes, it's only a game, but it's America's game, and the roots are deep. The Game has survived wars, the Great Depression, and a number of natural disasters. It has woven itself into the fabric of America. The Game set the stage for America to find itself racially and now provides the perfect setting, where merit alone dictates acceptance.

I'm grateful to all of the above and say a prayer of thanksgiving daily.

CONTENTS

FOREWORD

It was just another mid-June game at Ebbets Field so many adjectives ago, and I was sitting in the Dodgers dugout alongside Carl Erskine, who was to start against the Chicago Cubs. Small talk was the order of the day until Carl began to toss the game ball up in the air.

"I wonder what this little ball has in store for me today," Carl mused aloud. Two hours later I shared his joy as he pitched his first no-hitter, which would have been a perfect game had he not walked a most imperfect hitter, opposing pitcher Willard Ramsdell. It was one of Carl's two no-hitters during a brilliant career that saw him win 20 games in 1953, strike out 14 Yankees in a World Series game, win 122 games in a splendid 12-year career, and earn the respect and admiration of his teammates and opponents—which might have been his greatest accomplishment.

Carl was also involved in a numerical believe-it-or-not. On October 5, he was selected to pitch Game 5 of the 1952 World Series against the New York Yankees. Before the game, if memory serves me right, he received a telegram from the mayor of Fort Worth, Texas, where Carl pitched in his minor league days, congratulating Carl and Betty on their fifth wedding anniversary. I collected the three fives in my memory bank and watched somewhat in disbelief as the Yankees scored five runs in the fifth inning. Carl, however, was in no mood to let the Yankees ruin his party, as he hung tough, went 11 innings to win, 6-5. Oh, one other thing. When the game ended, I swear it was 5 after 5 p.m. As Ring Lardner used to say, "You could look it up."

The little man from Anderson, Indiana, was a very big man indeed back in those lovely days in Brooklyn, and it was with great fondness that the pure sound of Erskine was turned into the raucous "Oisk." Carl Erskine was always dependable, prepared, consistent, and businesslike, with a change-up that brought many a good hitter right out of his shoes. He pitched his game like a banker filling out your loan application, with preciseness and care. It was no surprise then to those who know him that he would one day wind up doing just that. However, you will not be getting a dry banker's report from this book, but rather the warm memories of a lovely man.

Nor, for that matter, would Carl complete the line, "See the Boys of Summer . . . *in their ruin.* No maudlin man is he. Not now, not ever. For he is more like the sundial that only records the sunlit hours.

Here, then, are some of those golden moments, the shared laughter and thrills, the pure joy of being a big leaguer . . . better yet, of being a Dodger.

Pull up a chair, get close to the dugout, and stay a while.

—*Vin Scully*

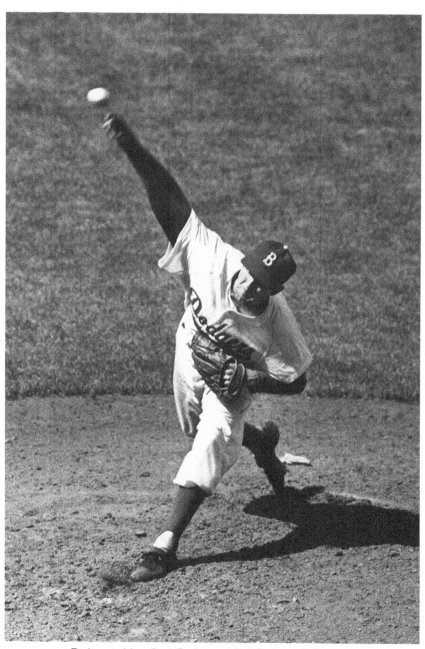

Delivered by Carl Erskine. *(Carl Erskine Collection)*

ACKNOWLEDGMENTS

In appreciation, I acknowledge several people who assisted and encouraged me in the writing of this book: Mark Langill and the Dodgers for research, editing, and file photos. Mary Lou Fadely, my secretary, who had to decipher many pages of my longhand. The Hall of Fame for photos. Vin Scully, Duke Snider, Rachel Robinson, Ed Roebuck, and Roger Kahn, all part of the Dodger family, who helped verify these happenings. And then my wife, Betty, who shared the excitement and challenges of these years with me.

INTRODUCTION

There is an old saying: "You can no more tell something you don't know than you can come back from someplace you've never been." Over time, I have been asked thousands of questions about the Brooklyn Dodgers, Ebbets Field, and the wonderful baseball era when New York City had three major league teams. I've also been asked about the historic move to Los Angeles. Often in relating the many fascinating events that took place during my career, in describing the personalities and retelling the bizarre, humorous, sometimes heartwarming stories, I've also been asked, "Are all of your stories true?" I say, "Yes, I couldn't possibly make them up the way they actually happened." I can tell these stories because I was there.

What I did was soak up, like a sponge, all of the atmosphere around me. I was so grateful to be in the big leagues—playing for a great team, living out my baseball career with close friends such as The Duke, Preacher, Pee Wee, Campy, Jackie, Hodges, Furillo, Newcombe, Clem Labine, and the rest of the cast of characters—I just naturally didn't miss much. Everybody on the scene was an important character: the grounds crew, the ushers, the ticket takers, the elevator boys, the special cops, the umpires, and, of course, the fans.

The following pages relate true events that took place during my career. I take great delight in telling and retelling them. After all, each one involves a friend or a baseball enemy, and at this mellow stage of my life, it's hard to tell them apart. I loved them all. Thanks for being a baseball fan with whom I can share my stories.

TALES FROM THE
DODGERS
DUGOUT

THE TALES

"Oisk"

I often get mail from young fans who say, "I didn't see you pitch, but my grandfather did." Then they ask where I got my nickname, "Oisk." Of course, that's a foreign language—"Brooklynese." The Brooklyn faithful pronounced Carl Erskine "Cal Oyskin," eventually shortened with yells from the very close Ebbets Field stands to "Hey, Oisk, I'm witcha babe, trow it tru his head," or, on a bad day, "Trade 'im to the Jints."

Baseball Scripture

Every profession has its own lingo, phrases, or inside nicknames, and baseball is no exception. A *clothesline* is a hard-hit line drive. A *tater* is a home run. A *wet one* is a spitball. *Sack* means base. *Lumber* is a bat. *Pill* is a baseball. *Smoke* is a fastball. *Can of corn* is an easy fly ball. *The eagle flies* is payday. *To undress him* means to throw him a high, tight pitch.

When I arrived in the "big leagues," I quickly caught on to most of the lingo. However, one phrase escaped me, and I was reluctant to ask what it meant. One of our coaches, when talking about a certain hitter, would refer to him as a *bible hitter*.

When I finally asked Elwin "Preacher" Roe what that meant, he said, "That means that feller is a dead first-ball hitter: Thou shall not pass."

What's a Baseball?

Well, the old "horsehide" is now cowhide, and in the center is a small ball of cork and rubber. Around this is wound wool and cotton thread. The cover has 108 red stitches, and for decades, it was hand-stitched. Today's balls are machine-stitched.

The umpires are required to rub up six dozen balls before each game. The substance used to rub the balls is Mississippi Mud. This clay-like mud actually comes from a river in the Delaware Water Gap in Maryland.

During World War II, fans were asked to return foul balls to the playing field, where they were collected in red, white, and blue barrels and sent to servicemen around the world for their teams and for general recreation. If a fan refused to throw the ball back, he was roundly booed as an unpatriotic lout.

In the postwar years, foul balls were kept by the fans. In fact, some stadiums, such as Sportsman's Park in St. Louis, gave a fan who caught a foul ball a Cardinals contract.

We always marveled at the businessman in a high-priced suit who would dive in the aisle on his hands and knees, scrapping for a baseball worth only a couple of dollars.

As a kid, I was told that baseball was the hardest sport to play. You had a round bat and a round ball. The object of the game was to hit the ball square.

The Red Thread

Branch Rickey, a devout Christian and president of the Brooklyn Dodgers, was a master psychologist and used these skills in talking with his players, either in group sessions or, often, one on one.

I recall one of my early sessions with Mr. Rickey. He asked a lot of questions—not about baseball, but about personal matters. Then he surprised me when he asked: "Do you go to church?" When I responded yes, he said, "Well, I encourage that, and here's why: I find that any individual who will so discipline his life to sit regularly in a place of worship and think on the teachings of Christ, that person will develop a quiet self-confidence that will stand him in good stead, no matter what pressures life brings to him. That faith is like a red thread that runs through every part of people's lives—no matter if they are a baseball player, a truck driver, a housewife. It makes no difference. They'll have it."

There were times during my career, in a pressure situation on the mound, when I would get renewed confidence when I looked at the baseball I was holding and saw those red stitches.

It's All in the Delivery

During the 1930s, 1940s, and 1950s, baseball witnessed many historic changes. The game has prided itself on instituting very few rules changes in its 100-plus-year history; however, around the edges, just look at what happened.

Baseball was traditionally a day game. Lights were first used in Cincinnati and Brooklyn in the mid-1930s. Baseball had always been a bus and train game. The Dodgers introduced flying by using a DC-3 to fly the team around Florida during spring training in the early 1950s. In time, the Dodgers bought their own plane and hired their own flight crew. Eventually, the jet plane keyed baseball's expansion to the West Coast.

Baseball had also been a radio game. In the late 1940s, television was introduced, and baseball thus became a sport that could be watched as well as heard from afar.

From its inception, baseball had always been a racially segregated sport. True, the Negro Leagues existed, but no man of color played in "professional baseball" (i.e., minor or major league baseball) alongside white players until Branch Rickey introduced Jackie Robinson to the world.

Over the Top

I've often been asked how I became a baseball pitcher and, more specifically, how I came to throw straight overhand. Only a very few pitchers I saw in the big leagues threw straight overhand. Warren Spahn and Sandy Koufax were two Hall of Famers who did.

Well, I was the youngest of three boys, so when my dad (who loved to throw) and my two older brothers, Lloyd and Donald, would play catch at the side of our house, I was the one who would get the heat. We played a game called burnout. You start tossing nice and easy, and then each throw gets a little harder. When they finally pinned me back against the barn, I would grit my teeth and reach as high as I could to throw harder. I threw the hardest straight overhand.

Another question I often get asked is how I learned to throw the overhand curve. (Old-timers called it a *drop*.) My dad had a baseball book, and one evening in our living room he got the book and a baseball and was showing me how to put curveball rotation on a pitch. As he stood in the middle of the room—the book in his left hand and ball in his right, he was demonstrating the delivery. Suddenly, he made a full arm motion and accidentally released the ball. It bounced once and then went through the open doorway into the dining room.

We then heard this huge crash when it hit the glass of my mother's china cupboard. Glass seemed to fall for five minutes.

My mother screamed, "Matt Erskine! What have you done?"

My dad, with a smirk on his face, said to me, "Son, that's the biggest break I ever got on a curveball."

"If at First . . ."

After high school graduation in 1945, I was drafted into the U.S. Navy. World War II was in full swing. When boot camp was over, I was stationed at Boston Navy Yard. The 1946 baseball season had started, so I went to the recreation officer, introduced myself, and asked if I could get on the baseball team. The officer seemed a little indifferent, and then asked me my name and where I had ever played. I told him I had pitched in high school and semipro in Indiana. He looked me over, asked me what I weighed—the answer was 165—and then said he had enough pitchers. I went away disappointed and found a local semipro team to pitch for on Sundays.

My discharge came a few weeks later, and I signed with the Dodgers and spent the next year and a half in the minors. By 1948 I was in the majors. I pitched a night game against the St. Louis Cardinals and won. The next night, during the pregame workout, a man kept yelling at me from the stands. Players were not permitted to fraternize on the field with the fans, so I ignored him. Still, the fan persisted in calling out to me. Finally, I walked over to the rail. He stuck out his hand and said, "Shake hands with the dumbest so-and-so in the world. I'm the rec officer who wouldn't let you pitch for the U.S. Navy. With guys like me, I'm surprised we won the war."

Double Bonus

Prior to the big-money era in baseball, it was rare that a signing bonus was ever paid to a player. It was customary to give a set of Grand Slam Louisville Slugger golf clubs or, to a really hot prospect, a new car. The automobile was either a Ford or a Chevrolet that cost between $700 and $800.

When several clubs, especially the Boston Braves, were attempting to sign me, Branch Rickey met me in the Kenmore Hotel in Boston while I was still in the navy and signed me to my first contract. I negotiated a $3,500 bonus—unheard of in 1946. That was more than my dad made all year working for a General Motors plant in Anderson, Indiana.

I was discharged two weeks later, on July 25, and played the balance of the season with a Dodger farm team in Danville, Illinois. A.B. "Happy" Chandler, then the baseball commissioner, called me to his Cincinnati office in October and said he was declaring me a free agent because the Dodgers had violated his directive prohibiting the signing of a player while still in the military. The bidding started again, so I asked Mr. Rickey for an additional $5,000 and got it.

Ten years later I was in the middle of my big-league career and happened to pitch a no-hitter against the Giants, May 12, 1956. Dizzy Dean was broadcasting *The Game of the Week*. He interviewed me after the game.

"Who signed you?" he asked. "Branch Rickey," I said. "Cheapest man who ever lived," said Dizzy. "I played for him at St. Louis. He paid peanuts—two bags a week," he said. When I told him about the two bonuses, he turned to the camera and said, "Folks, this here young man deserves to be in the Hall of Fame. Not only because he pitched two no-hitters, but because he got two bonuses from Branch Rickey."

Love Bug

I once played in a benefit golf tournament in Fort Wayne, Indiana. At the big reception before dinner, a young lady approached me and announced, "Hello, Carl Erskine, I was once madly in love with you." Before I could respond, she pulled out a snapshot from her purse. There I was at age 19 in my Danville, Illinois, uniform—I was playing for the Dodgers' affiliate in the Three-I League. I was standing, and next to me was a little 10-year-old girl who was seated on top of the dugout at a stadium in Terre Haute, Indiana, the home of the Phillies' farm team. She told me, "My daddy used to let me and my girlfriends attend the game there, and you were always so nice to us."

The woman was Mari Hulman, the daughter of Indianapolis Motor Speedway owner Tony Hulman. Both of her parents have passed away, and it is her voice that starts the Greatest Spectacle in Racing when she says, "Ladies and gentlemen, start your engines."

Cool It

Being a minor league player in the pre–air-conditioning days was a hot and humid experience. After one sweltering night game in Evansville, Indiana (of the Three-I League—Indiana, Illinois, Iowa), my roommate, Bernie Zender, was having a tough night sleeping. The VenDome Hotel was small and had few windows. Some of our players would take cold showers and go to bed wet.

Bernie went one better. I came to our room one night and found him sleeping in the bathtub. His head was on a pillow at the slanting end, and the water was up to his chin.

At age 19 I was proud to be in a Dodger uniform in my first year of professional baseball in Danville, Illinois. *(Carl Erskine Collection)*

The Decision

There are times in life when one decision can change the course of the rest of your life. It happened to me on Grand Stadium's pitching mound in Havana, Cuba, in February 1947.

I was 20 years old and had just finished my first season in the minors. The Dodgers sent me to Havana to pitch in a winter league.

I was told in my first year that if I wanted to make it to the big leagues, I had to change the way I gripped my curve. As I worked on the new grip and delivery in Cuba, I could not get much velocity on the pitch, so in tight situations I would revert back to my old curve. This went on for several games.

My next start was against Alamendares, and I had them shut out 3-0 through eight innings. In Havana a shutout meant a $25 bonus, so I was determined to keep my opponent scoreless. But in the ninth inning, the leadoff man, Dee Fondy, tripled. With Fondy on third and no outs, I faced the big question: Do I stay with my new curveball or go back to my old reliable pitch to save the shutout? I was torn. I massaged the resin bag, turning over both sides of the debate in my head. I wanted the shutout, but I wanted long-term success too. Finally I said to myself, "No, I am not giving in. I'm sticking with my new curveball." I retired the next three batters and stranded Fondy on third base.

Yes, I got the shutout and the $25, but I received much more than that. I matured as a pitcher, and that experience did wonders for my self-confidence. By July 1948 I had won 15 games in Double A in Fort Worth, and the Dodgers came calling.

With me (far right) are Monte Basgall, Fred Meagher, Lefty Gomez, Dino Restelli, and Solly Hemus when we played in the Cuban winter league. *(Carl Erskine Collection)*

The Commissioners

The commissioner of baseball is a highly prestigious office but carries with it the potential for controversy. The first commissioner, Kennesaw Mountain Landis, was chosen by the owners to help erase the stigma caused by the "Black Sox Scandal" in 1919 where it was suspected that some Chicago White Sox players had been bribed to throw one or more World Series games. The players were banned from the game for life, and Landis was to rule with an iron hand and re-establish the purity of the game.

Players have usually viewed the commissioners as the owners' commissioner, because the owners select and hire each commissioner. From 1945 to 1951, A.B. "Happy" Chandler, the former governor of Kentucky, was the commissioner. "Happy" Chandler was a very visible commissioner and was often seen at games, in major league clubhouses, and at numerous social functions on behalf of baseball. He eventually became known as the players' commissioner, chiefly because he supported Branch Rickey and the integration of baseball. He also was instrumental in getting the owners to fund a respectable pension plan for players.

From 1951 to 1965, Ford Frick, a former sportswriter, served as commissioner. Frick was reserved, quiet, and rather nonvisible as commissioner. I was once summoned to his office and called on the carpet for being quoted in the New York press that "if Commissioner Frick walked into a major league clubhouse, the players wouldn't know him." He challenged me on that statement and soon after that sent his assistant Fred Flagg to make regular clubhouse visits on his behalf.

Years later I did a radio interview with Chandler. At one point I asked him what he thought of his successor. Chandler answered, "He slept longer than Rip Van Winkle."

Four Managers

I played for four different managers in my career, all of them well known and successful. And each one had a different philosophy of managing.

Familiar to most is Leo Durocher, famous for his assertion, "Nice guys finish last." Burt Shotton replaced Durocher after Leo was suspended in 1948. Burt was a real gentleman who, like the immortal Connie Mack, managed in his street clothes.

In our clubhouse meetings, Burt would give us his pep talk, then finish by saying, "Fellows, I saved my money and bought savings bonds. I got mine; now go out there and get yours."

Charlie Dressen, a one-man operator, was a take-charge manager. He seldom sought the advice of his coaches or anyone else. When we were behind in a game, Charlie would pace up and down the dugout. He'd say, "You guys hold 'em; I'll think of somethin'."

Then came Walter Alston, a man of few words. In fact, in 1954, his first season as manager of the Dodgers, the sportswriters came to me, asking, "How do we write anything? He won't talk." They finally learned that he did talk—when he had something to say.

The team got off to a slow start that spring, after having had a great year in 1953. Finally, prior to a spring training game in Jacksonville, Walt held a team meeting. He's a rookie manager talking to a veteran team of Pee Wee Reese, Gil Hodges, Jackie Robinson, Roy Campanella, Duke Snider, etc. He said, "I've read a lot of clippings about how great this team is. I haven't seen it. You guys are pros—you know what it takes to win. I don't give pep talks. You either do it, or we get someone else! Meeting's over."

The next year, Walt brought Brooklyn its only World Series championship.

Branch Rickey: "Let's Make a Deal"

M r. Rickey was a genius at judging talent, and he had a lot to look at when his 26 farm teams were all in spring training at Vero Beach, Florida. Dodgertown was like a baseball college, with hundreds of players throwing, hitting, playing intrasquad games, and doing baseball drills. At night, after the evening meal, Mr. Rickey would assemble his many scouts and minor league managers in a large room where the walls were lined with blackboards. Each board had one of the minor league team names written across the top. The purpose of the meeting was to select who could best fit teams from Class D to Class Triple A. It was a competitive session for the managers, who all wanted the best players they could get. Mr. Rickey would read a name and give some stats, and then discussion would follow. Each manager was eager to talk about why a particular good player was right for his team.

Finally, Mr. Rickey read the name of a young pitcher who had talent but was difficult to handle and had a reputation for being disruptive on a team. No manager spoke up. Mr. Rickey read some of his stats, which were pretty good. Still no takers. The session seemed stalled. Just then, the phone rang; another National League owner was calling Mr. Rickey to talk about a player deal. He needed pitchers. As Mr. Rickey stood in front of the scouts and managers, he began to extol the virtues of this young pitcher. In a matter of a few minutes, Mr. Rickey sold him to the other owner for $30,000—a great deal of money in 1948. He hung up the phone, looked at his player list, and said, "Who's next?"

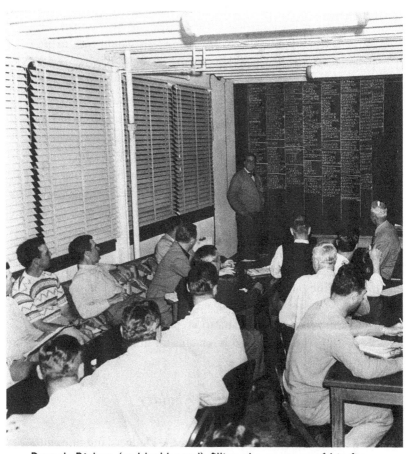

Branch Rickey (at blackboard) filling the rosters of his farm clubs at a 1950 meeting in Dodgertown. In the foreground at the far left (wearing a striped shirt) is Bobby Bragan. *(Courtesy of the Dodgers)*

Saved

At Vero Beach, Florida, on the old naval air station that Branch Rickey leased for Dodger spring training, there was a public beach that the players would rush to after practice. The ocean there has a really strong undertow, and we very quickly learned how dangerous it was out there.

Bobby Morgan, a classy infielder, was out in the ocean, enjoying the sun, when he got caught in the undertow and was being pulled out to sea. He couldn't swim against the current but was able to grab onto a piling that was protruding out of the water. He hung on for his life, wrapping his legs and arms around the piling. He called for help.

Gene Hermanski plunged in and swam out to him. He brought Morgan back to shore and saved his life.

When Morgan was taken back to training camp, the trainers doctored all of the cuts on his body from the barnacles that were on the piling. For the next several days, he looked like he had been beaten with a cat o' nine tails.

Of course, the organization prohibited Dodger players from using the beach, and it remains off limits to this day.

Mr. Rickey Salary

Tommy Lasorda and I were in the Dodgers' minor leagues during the Branch Rickey era. Mr. Rickey was well respected, and he influenced, for the good, most of the 790 players in the Dodger system.

Mr. Rickey, however, was very frugal and seldom let his players and big salaries get close together. We were all young and hungry and also very glad to be in pro baseball. Whenever you entered his office to negotiate your contract after a particularly good year, Mr. Rickey, using great psychology, might say,

Catcher Roy Campanella and Dodgers president Branch Rickey negotiate a contract. *(Courtesy of the Dodgers)*

"Well, son, you had a nice year. We've decided to let you come back."

Tommy says that after he and Mr. Rickey agreed to a salary one year, Mr. Rickey said it was better to keep the amount "just between us." Tommy claims he said to Mr. Rickey, "You don't have to worry about me saying anything to anyone about my salary. I'm just as ashamed of it as you are."

Bobby Bragan

Mr. Rickey had a brilliant mind for baseball and strong moral and religious views. He used his station in life to promote proper and ethical values and lifestyles, as when he founded the Fellowship of Christian Athletes.

Mr. Rickey was also extremely tight with team expenses. With his organization in charge of such a far-reaching number of minor league teams—each reporting daily about its performance via Western Union telegram—the cost was getting out of hand. Mr. Rickey issued a directive insisting that reports be kept to a minimum of words.

A couple of days later, Mr. Rickey wired Bobby Bragan at his Fort Worth, Texas, Double A team, inquiring about me and whether Bragan thought I was ready for the majors. Bobby, knowing and respecting Mr. Rickey, wired back a one-word reply: "Yes."

When Mr. Rickey received the wire that afternoon, he was puzzled and wired Bragan back saying, "Yes, what?" Bobby replied, "Yes, Sir."

A Glove in the Hand Is Worth . . . ?

My second year in professional baseball was in Fort Worth, Texas. Bob Storey, the owner of Nakona Leather Goods, approached me to sign a contract endorsing Nakona baseball gloves. I was flattered to get my first chance to endorse a product. The deal offered me no money but two gloves a year. I signed.

Later that year I was called up to the Dodgers. Bob visited me and offered to let me out of the contract because he said I could probably sign with Rawlings or Wilson Sporting Goods for some real money. I thought about it a minute, recalling how thrilled I was when Bob signed me, and said, "Well, you signed me when I was a nobody, so if it's okay with you, I'll stay with Nakona."

When I got to Brooklyn, Bob sent me a couple of gloves. Nakona made a very heavy, very bulky ball glove. When my roomie Duke Snider first picked one up, he said, "Erskine, if you pitch using this glove, you'll have a sore left arm."

Over the years, Nakona has developed a first-class array of baseball gloves that are still in demand today.

For example, I was leaving the field during a benefit game one night in St. Petersburg, Florida, with several other former major leaguers when a man in the front box seat kept yelling at me. After a couple of innings of persistence, I walked over and asked him what he wanted. "I want to buy your glove," he said. "I can't sell you my glove," I said, "I'm using it." "I'll give you a hundred dollars for it," he retorted. I just walked away.

The next inning he yelled and held up two fingers. I ignored him. A few minutes later he yelled again and held up three fingers. I was in the dugout, so I asked the batboy if he knew the guy. The batboy said he was a dentist from Clearwater and a reputable collector. I looked right at the batboy and said, "If he goes to four hundred, he's going to own this Nakona." Sure enough, a few minutes later the guy yelled and held up four fingers.

I walked out and stood in front of him.

"You got cash?" I asked.

"Yes."

"Look me over real good. What else do you like? Shoes? Cap? Belt?" He wasn't interested.

I wrote Nakona for a new glove and told them they were underpriced because I had just gotten $400 for mine.

Forbes Field

I was called to the Dodgers on Sunday, July 25, 1948. I joined the team in Pittsburgh. They were staying at the Schenley Hotel. After I checked in, I wanted to go to the ballpark, get a locker, and be ready for game time. I was pretty nervous because I didn't know anyone on the big club. When I walked out onto the big porch of the Schenley, most of the Dodgers were sitting out there relaxing. I reluctantly approached the players and said, "How do I get to Forbes Field?" Aware that I was a greenhorn, they said, "Oh, you take a cab." So I walked down the front steps, hailed a taxi, and got in. The cabbie said, "Where to?" I said, "Forbes Field." He looked back at me and said, "What?" I knew something was fishy. Then I looked up at the porch. The whole team was having a big laugh. Forbes Field was only half a block around the corner from the Schenley.

Shuba

My first win in the majors came on July 25, 1948—the same day I joined the Dodgers. I relieved Hugh Casey late in the game. I was a little wild and walked a couple of hitters before Ralph Kiner hit a sinking line drive to left field. George Shuba made a great shoestring catch to double Johnny Hopp off first base and get me out of the inning. We went on to win the game by scoring in the ninth.

Years later, at a Brooklyn Dodger reunion, I saw Shuba, who, incidentally, was a pure left-handed hitter but a little shaky with the glove. I said, "George, did I ever thank you for that great shoestring catch off Kiner to help me win my first game?"

George said, "Yeah, I remember that play. I trapped the ball."

Hanson Place YMCA

When I was called up to the Brooklyn Dodgers, I was only making $425 per month, so I couldn't afford to check into a hotel. Having been raised around the YMCA in Anderson, Indiana, I asked where the "Y" was in Brooklyn. I was told the Hanson Place YMCA was the largest "Y" in the world. I went there and checked in. My room was located in a small corner on the second floor. It had a desk and a cot. The shower and restrooms were down the hall, along with a pay telephone.

Over the next few days I won two games in relief and had the thrill of calling home on that pay phone to tell the good news. Then I won my next three starts and was 5-0. Each time, I'd make that exciting phone call to my mom and dad.

Years later, after I was well established as a starting pitcher and my salary got into five figures, Betty and I and our kids lived in Bay Ridge in a nice row house owned by Mrs. Grace Coglin. Whenever I got into a pitching slump, I was tempted to go back and check into the Hanson Place "Y" to get straightened out.

Hermanski

In 1948, baseball owners agreed to institute a minimum major league salary. It was set at $5,000 per season. Believe it or not, the salaries of a multitude of major leaguers had to be raised in order to get them up to the minimum.

My first roommate was Gene Hermanski, a left-handed-hitting outfielder with good power and a somewhat unsteady glove. It so happened that in an afternoon game at Ebbets Field, Hermanski dropped a fly ball in left field that cost the Dodgers a ballgame. When Gene and I went to our room at the St. George Hotel in Brooklyn, he was very distressed. The phone rang, and it was Branch Rickey. He requested that Gene be in his office at 10 the next morning. This was very bad news, and Gene took it very hard. He knew he was gone—traded, sold, or possibly released. He fretted all night long.

The next morning he left the hotel for 215 Montague Street to meet Mr. Rickey. I felt sorry for Gene but wished him good luck. In about an hour he was back, grinning from ear to ear and happy as a clam. "Carl, you can't believe what happened," he gushed. "When I went in to Mr. Rickey's office, he said, 'Sit down, son.' Then he called to his secretary, Jane Ann: 'Come in here. This boy is under the minimum, so we've got to raise him a thousand dollars.'"

Gene stayed with the Dodgers and, in 1949, led the club in home runs. I also saw him make a great catch to start a rare triple play.

Hit and Run

Currently, only two big-league ballparks remain from my pitching days—Yankee Stadium and Wrigley Field. Both are classic ballparks—not for their architecture,

After my first start, some teammates—Bruce Edwards, me, Gene Hermanski, manager Burt Shotton, Pee Wee Reese, and Marvin Rackley—celebrate Hermanski's three home runs. *(Carl Erskine Collection)*

but for all of the remarkable events that have happened in each, or in the case of Chicago Cubs' home, what hasn't happened there since 1904, their last world championship.

Wrigley, however, was the backdrop for two memorable moments in my career—one of them is my first at-bat in 1948.

Catching that day for the Cubs was Mickey Owens, and umpiring home plate was Larry Goetz. I took my stance in the batter's box and watched the first pitch, a fastball, whiz by.

"Strike one," Goetz called. I backed out of the batter's box, looked right at Goetz, and said to him, "The pitch was inside."

Owens stood up, parting Goetz and me, and said, "Son, this man is going to be calling balls and strikes for you. Don't question his judgment. Get in there and bat."

I was never sure if Owens was trying to help a rookie out or score some points with the ump for himself.

The second incredible event at Wrigley came later in my career when Jackie Robinson doubled off left center field's ivy-covered wall. When he slid into second base, he banged his knee on the bag. He hobbled around second base a bit, in obvious pain. From the bench, Walt Alston said, "Hey, Erskine, go run for Jackie."

Now occasionally I was called on to pinch run—but I never thought it would be for Jackie Robinson.

"Colorless"

As I've gotten older (I turned 77 on December 13, 2003), I've appreciated the perspective of looking back and seeing how things in life connect.

I lived on the west side of Anderson, Indiana, and had some neighborhood buddies. One was an African American named Johnny Wilson. We were both poor kids but liked sports and played together year-round from elementary school

Neighborhood buddies from Anderson, Indiana (left to right): me, Johnny Wilson, and Jack Rector. All three went into professional sports. *(Carl Erskine Collection)*

through high school. Johnny was particularly great in basketball. We were together a lot and were great buddies.

Johnny became Mr. Basketball in Indiana after leading his high school team to the 1946 state championship. He later played basketball for the Harlem Globetrotters and baseball for the Chicago American Giants in the Negro Leagues. One of my great memories is the day in Pittsburgh when I beat the Pirates, 5-1. Johnny was in the stands. We sat out in Schenley Park after the game and talked.

We said, "Boy, look at us—the big time from the old neighborhood." That night, Johnny was playing for the Chicago American Giants.

I say all this because of what happened at Ebbets Field in 1948. I came out of the Dodger clubhouse after a game and stopped to chat with some of the wives. Among them was Rachel Robinson with Jackie Jr. This was a protected area inside wrought-iron fencing, so the fans were pressing against the fence, peering in as the players came out of the clubhouse.

The next day Jackie came to my locker and said, "I want to thank you for what you did yesterday." I was puzzled. "You know," he said, "you stopped out there in front of all those fans and talked with Rachel and little Jack."

I said, "Hey, Jackie, you can congratulate me on a well pitched game, but not for that." That was just a natural thing for me to do.

You see, my experience with Johnny Wilson prepared me well for my nine seasons with Jackie. Johnny taught me to be color-blind.

The Real Story

M r. Rickey was a genius at reading not only the talent of baseball prospects, but also their attitude and aptitude. This genius is what led Mr. Rickey to his greatest achievement—finding Jackie Robinson and coaching him so that he could hurdle the color barrier in baseball and ultimately be elected to baseball's Hall of Fame. However, even that accomplishment pales in comparison to Jackie's impact on America in its struggle to allow every citizen the same civil rights. Jackie proved he belonged, and he helped to open hearts and minds.

Now, how did Branch Rickey single out this hot-blooded, gifted athlete? As a four-sport letterman at UCLA, Robinson showed everyone that he could play, but so could dozens of other black players. Branch Rickey came at it from a different direction. As a farm boy in southern Ohio, he was raised by a strong Christian mother who made her son promise that he wouldn't abandon his faith when he went into this roughshod business of pro baseball. His research told him that Jackie, too, had been raised by a strong Christian mother who instilled in Jackie the virtues of discipline and respect for every individual. Also, Jackie was educated, a college man at a time when baseball had few college men. His intelligence would help him understand the significance of Mr. Rickey's attempt to break from tradition.

One thing Branch Rickey desired of his players was that they be married. When Mr. Rickey met Rachel, Jackie's wife, a beautiful, intelligent college nursing graduate, he must have thought, "This is my man."

The foundation for this momentous move was laid when, during a private meeting with Jackie, Mr. Rickey gave him a word picture of the physical and mental abuse he would face. Then Mr. Rickey pulled from his desk drawer a volume, Pepini's *Life of Christ*, and read to Jackie the parable of "turning the other cheek."

"The bully is done," Mr. Rickey said, "when your only retaliation is a nonviolent response." As history would show, Mr. Rickey picked the right man.

Branch Rickey instructs Jackie Robinson to "turn the other cheek." *(Carl Erskine Collection)*

Hugh Casey

U ntil the early 1950s, major league teams did not have pitching coaches, or at least coaches who had once been pitchers; consequently, young pitchers relied on the older, experienced pitchers for counsel and advice.

Hugh Casey offered me this sound advice when I joined the Dodgers. "Son," he said, "there are guys in this league who hit .340 every year. They hit all pitchers, and they're gonna hit you. My advice is to really bear down on the guys ahead of these good hitters in the lineup. Keep those weak sisters off the base. Then when Musial and Mize get their hits, you don't get hurt." Second, he said, "There are things in this league you can't change: the weather on the day you pitch, the park you're pitching in, and the umpire calling balls and strikes. So forget these things and concentrate on what you have control of. Keep your fastball in good spots and your curveball down and away. Kid, you'll win some games."

Now, Hugh Casey wasn't necessarily a spiritual man. However, he did use a lot of theological language in giving me this good advice.

The Lesson

D uring the late 1940s and early 1950s, the Pittsburgh Pirates had a strong-hitting lineup headed by Hall of Famer Ralph Kiner. Although the Pirates were buried in the second division, the fans came out in big numbers to see Ralph Kiner hit home runs. Twice he hit more than 50 homers in a season; six times he hit more than 40.

After the Pirates had lost a Sunday doubleheader, we arrived in Pittsburgh to start a series on a Monday. The headline in the Pittsburgh Press read, "Pirates lose two," with the kicker, "Who cares? Kiner hits three."

When I was a rookie, I was called in to pitch to Ralph Kiner with the bases loaded and nobody out. The crowd was really charged up for this scene—the mighty Kiner facing this scared kid pitcher. Yes, I was a little shook up. I forgot Mr. Rickey's advice about inner control. The crowd was chanting for Kiner to hit one.

I'm here to tell you I didn't disappoint that big crowd. Kiner hit one out into the night for a grand slam.

The next day Mr. Rickey told me I was being sent to the Dodgers' Triple A team in Montreal. I pitched well there and was recalled in a few weeks. Mr. Rickey asked me if I knew why I was sent back to the minors. I said, "Oh, yes, that home run to Kiner."

"No," he said. "After the home run, you stuck out your chin and retired the side on 11 pitches. That's why you were no longer intimidated—you were mad. Had you pitched that way to Kiner, you would have avoided the home run. I hope you learned that important lesson."

Mr. Rickey's Parable

According to Bobby Bragan, Mr. Rickey always finished his Dodgertown managers' meeting with an illustration that had great impact on the present circumstances, giving his staff something to remember.

Managers were often assigned to cities that were new to them, which was the reason for Mr. Rickey's parable.

"A fellow got off at the train station in a town where he had never been before. He asked an old gentleman sitting there, 'What kind of a town is this?' The old gentleman replied, 'What kind of town did you come from?' 'Oh, it was a hard town, greedy people all looking out for themselves. It was a tough town.'

"Just then, another fellow came by and asked the old man, 'What kind of town is this?' Again, his reply was this same question: 'What kind of town did you come from?' 'Well,' he said, 'it was a great town—friendly people all willing to help. It was a very generous town.'"

Mr. Rickey then said, "Managers, you'll be the ones to make the kinds of towns you're going to."

Nairy a Whisker

At Ebbets Field, my locker was just across from Roy Campanella. We were close enough that as we dressed or undressed, we could easily talk to one another. Often we kidded, told a joke, or talked family. The clubhouse before a game was an easy, relaxed atmosphere. It was later that we got serious.

I was always fascinated by how Roy shaved. He kept a large tube of Nair, the white creamy lotion that women used to take hair off their legs, in his locker. Campy would spread a coat of it over his face and neck and then sit and read the paper for several minutes. He would then go into the trainer's room, get a tongue depressor, and, as if using an old-fashioned straight razor, would scrape all of the Nair and whiskers off his face. His face was as smooth as a baby's bottom, and the shave would last him over a week.

After watching his ritual, I decided I would try it one day. I asked Roy for a small dab and placed the Nair on my chin. I waited—but not for long. The lotion burned. I thought it was going to sear a hole in my chin. I wiped it off quickly and never looked back.

My next shave was Gilette.

Hatten in Relief

Rex Barney was a sensational, hard-throwing Dodger pitcher. He also had an awesome curveball. His only trouble was his lack of control. He could be, and often was, extremely wild, sometimes not making it out of the first inning. If he did, however, he often went on to pitch a low-hit game, registering many strikeouts.

In a day game at Ebbets Field, Rex was to be the starting pitcher. Burt Shotton, our manager, called me aside and said, "Look, when Rex starts the game, I want you to start throwing in the bullpen. If he gets into trouble early, you're my pitcher. You start throwing at the start of each inning. I'll not go very far with Barney."

So in the first inning Rex walks the bases full, and I'm heating up like crazy. Rex blows a couple of guys away on strikes and gets out of the inning. The second inning was much like the first: I was throwing and staying ready for the call, but Rex got out of the inning. This went on through eight innings. For eight innings I threw pitch for pitch with Barney. In the ninth, with a one-run lead, Shotton sent word to get Joe Hatten, a southpaw, up, too, so he had both a right- and a left-handed pitcher ready. Sure enough, Rex had a shaky start in the ninth. After two were out, he walked his third batter to load the bases. Shotton sent coach Clyde Sukeforth to the mound to make a pitching change. Because the next hitter was left-handed, Sukey brought in the lefty, Joe Hatten. Joe retired the batter on three pitches for a Dodger win.

The next day, at the end of our team meeting before game time, Burt was making the bullpen assignments. He said, "Hatten, you're in the pen." Then he said, "Oh, no, you pitched yesterday. Erskine, you're it."

White Horses

The Dodger bullpen in Ebbets Field was down the right field line in foul territory, with the stands running close beside it. The kids would constantly come to the railing and beg for one of the brand-new baseballs resting in a catcher's mitt on the bench, waiting to be used for warmups.

After being pestered for several innings, our bullpen coach, Clyde Sukeforth, would slowly get up, casually spit a little tobacco juice to the side and then step over to the railing, holding a new baseball. The kids got very excited. Then Clyde, in his slow-paced and best Waldoboro, Maine, Down East accent, would say, "Look, kids, I'd like to give you this baseball, but we've got a little problem right now. There's a real shortage of white horses to make these baseballs. That's why I can't give any away." The kids would look surprised, but they believed Clyde and quietly would leave.

Kids Know

It's always a special experience when kids ask for an autograph. And kids are usually so honest that you can tell how popular you are by how they seek your autograph.

My rookie year was especially exciting, because signing autographs for Brooklyn kids made me feel like a bona fide major league player. That is, until the day I came out of the Dodger clubhouse and was stopped by several boys wanting autographs. I signed several, and then one boy came back a second time. I gladly signed again. In a few minutes, he was back for a third autograph. This time I asked him why he would want three of my autographs. His honest answer was, "Actually, I would like to have six. If I can get six of yours, I can trade them for one of Jackie Robinson's."

B.H.G.

Connie Mack and Burt Shotton were the only two managers I knew who did not wear a baseball uniform during the game. Cornelius Alexander McGillicuddy, Mack's real name, managed the Philadelphia Athletics for more than 50 years. He didn't need to wear a uniform—he owned the team. Shotton, an outfielder during the Babe Ruth era, was a top scout for Mr. Rickey and the Dodgers before becoming a manager.

In 1948, Leo Durocher was suspended and fired, and Shotton became the interim manager. Shotton would sit on the bench and take notes during the game. Often a player would hit a hard line drive, only to have it caught for an easy out. He would come back to the bench cussing, throwing his bat, and bemoaning his bad luck. Shotton would just say, "That's okay, son. I saw that shot you hit, and I have a special column for that—B.H.G.—Balls Hit Good."

Brooklyn Bonus

During the 1940s and the 1950s, big-league salaries were quite low. Most of us found some kind of temporary work during the off season. Endorsements were also few and far between. However, there are a number of ways to be paid. In Brooklyn we were treated in a first-class manner. The neighborhoods we lived in were great to our families while we were on the road. We all had small children, and the neighbors gave the players a sense of security while we were away.

Another example was Abe Meyerson, the owner of a neighborhood deli in Bay Ridge. Every time I pitched, win or lose, Abe would appear at my door with two big bags of deli groceries. When I objected to this kind of generosity (Abe had five children of his own), Abe would say, "Hey, you guys deserve the best. Why, you shouldn't have to pay rent, utilities, buy groceries, or anything else. We love you guys here in Brooklyn."

Satchel

One of the really fabled characters in baseball history is a black pitcher named Leroy "Satchel" Paige. He started pitching before Jackie Robinson was born and was a superstar in the black major leagues before Jackie broke the color line. He was often associated with Hall of Famer Bob Feller in making postseason barnstorming trips, pitting a black team against an all-white major league team. Satch could pitch every day, had uncanny control, and threw a variety of pitches he called inshoots, outshoots, risers, and drops. All for strikes.

I once talked to Satchel and asked him to describe his "best stuff." In his unique speaking manner, he said, "Well, Cawl, I had a little piece o' fastball and a little piece o' curve, then a dab o' this and that."

In 1948 the Cleveland Indians signed him to a major league contract. He was 42 years old. His comment on aging: "How old would you be if you didn't know how old you was?" He also claimed to have a secret formula for liniment that gave his arm longevity. Satch won 28 major league games.

In 1965 Kansas City signed him, and at age 59, he pitched three scoreless innings in a major league game.

Satchel Paige's homespun wisdom is spelled out in his five rules for life:

1. "If your stomach disputes you, lie down and pacify it with cool thoughts."

2. "Keep the juices flowin' by janglin' 'round gently as you move."

3. "Go very lightly on the vices, such as carryin' on in society. The social ramble ain't restful."

Leroy "Satchel" Paige discusses the art of pitching and other topics. *(Courtesy of the Baseball Hall of Fame)*

4. "Avoid running at all times."

5. "Don't look back. Sumpthin' might be gainin' on you."

Billy

The infield of Gil Hodges at first, Jackie Robinson at second, and Pee Wee Reese at shortstop overshadowed the slick little third baseman of the Dodgers from 1948 to 1954. Day in and day out, Billy Cox was the best third baseman of his day. He had such quick hands that it seemed as though he had four gloves instead of one.

Billy was quiet and unassuming, but he could really grab (or snip) those hot shots down the line. Notice the glove in the lower right-hand side of the accompanying photo on p. 38. This was Billy's own glove, and it has only three fingers. Maybe that's why he was so quick.

Jethroe

Gil Hodges was a quiet, strong man who, with his great hands and reach, was the glue to the famous Boys of Summer infield of Jackie Robinson, Pee Wee Reese, and Billy Cox. Gil also always had his head in the game.

One of the early black players in the majors was Sam Jethroe, a switch-hitting speedster who was playing for the Braves. On a close play at first base, Sam stumbled and fell, but he was still safe. He sprawled past first base and was very slow getting up. The trainer ran out and for several minutes attended to Sam, who was barely able to stand. Finally, Sam waved the trainer away and stayed in the game. On the first pitch to the next hitter, Sam took off and stole second. The throw from Campanella went through into center field, and Sam sped all the way home to score. It was a kind of in-your-face maneuver.

Versatile Billy Cox, "The Glove Man." *(Carl Erskine Collection)*

In the next series in Brooklyn, I started against the Braves. When Jethroe came up, I happened to walk him on a 3-2 pitch. He was always a threat to run, so he was flexing his legs at first base like a racehorse at the starting gate. Gil came over to the mound and talked to me, casually taking the ball from me under the cover of his big first baseman's glove. Gil trotted back to his position at first. I stood behind the mound and was massaging the resin bag. As Sam stood a couple of feet off first, Hodges stepped in between Sam and the bag. Holding his big glove open toward Sam, Gil calmly said, "Hey, Sam, look what I've got."

Jimmy Gray

Jimmy Gray was a uniformed police officer assigned to Ebbets. He was a former lightweight boxing champion and had a face to prove it—pug nose and scars on his chin. He loved to talk boxing and had a gruff and commanding way of recalling some tough opponents he had beaten.

Once, during batting practice before a day game, I was shagging flies in left field and stepped over to the stands to speak to Jimmy. As we stood there talking in foul territory, Carl Furillo hit a shot toward us. It skipped once off the grass and hit Jimmy directly in the right jaw, knocking him flat. In an instant he bounced up, dukes raised, flailing away wildly at the guy who decked him. It took his brother, another special cop, and two ushers to quiet him down and convince him that he wasn't in the ring.

Signs

The mysterious art of giving and taking signs from the coach or the manager is at the heart of baseball strategy. Signs must be simple, quickly given, and well disguised.

Most signs are touches or swipes of the uniform, face, or cap. The sign means nothing unless it is preceded by the key. For example, if the key is touching the skin, then the sign that follows is the one that counts. There are countless combinations for take, bunt, hit-and-run, and steal signs.

Signs from the catcher are usually simple finger signs, also in disguise. An indicator, or key, also precedes the one that counts. The international basic signs for a pitcher are as follows: one finger = fastball; two fingers = curveball; three fingers = off speed. Then there are all of the other specialty pitches.

Pitchers have enough to worry about without having to learn a complicated set of signs. The toughest I ever had to learn were the scoreboard signs. In that system, the sign changes with the count on the batter. There are nine combinations of counts on a batter:

0-0	0-1	2-1
1-1	0-2	3-1
2-2	0-3	3-2
first	second	third
sign	sign	sign

Depending on the count, the first, the second, or the third sign the catcher gives is the one the pitcher takes as the actual sign.

You can be sure no opponent is going to steal these signs. The pitcher and catcher aren't even sure what's coming.

Chuck Connors

The Dodgertown baseball complex was opened in 1948, right after World War II. Branch Rickey leased the Naval Air Station facility in Vero Beach, Florida, for $1 per year and converted it to a spring training site. Some 790 signed players in the Dodger organization—both major leaguers and minor leaguers—passed through there each spring, from mid-February to the end of April, representing rosters of 26 farm teams as well as the big-league club.

There was a lot of evening time to spend, with only one ping-pong table, a pool table, and a jukebox available for entertainment. Fortunately, we had a true showman among us, minor league first baseman Chuck Connors. Chuck would entertain us nightly with card tricks, poems, jokes, or debates. He was also one of several Dodger first basemen who stayed in the minors because Gil Hodges was a fixture on the big club.

Once, Mr. Rickey called Chuck into his office for a conference, a routine invitation for all of his players sooner or later. Mr. Rickey always stressed the moral and spiritual discipline needed in life, especially in the pressure-packed arena of professional baseball.

Connors related his conversation with Mr. Rickey. "Son, do you smoke?" "No sir, Mr. Rickey." "Chuck, do you run around with fast women?" "No, sir." "Do you drink hard liquor?" Chuck swears he answered, "Mr. Rickey, if I have to drink to play for you, I want to be traded." Later, he was traded to the Cubs and then optioned to their Triple A team in Los Angeles before becoming, of course, a famous TV star known as "The Rifleman."

Gil Hodges

Gil Hodges came to the Dodgers as a catcher and then was converted to a first baseman. He had great hands and was a very smart player. He often learned the signs of opposing teams and would know when they were going to hit-and-run, bunt, or steal. Often he would call time, come to the mound, and say, "There's nobody out, a man on first—now don't throw to first, because I'll be charging to field this bunt; I got their sign." Sure enough, he'd get a great jump and foil their play.

Gil made a play against the Giants that none of us had ever seen or ever tried. Eddie Stanky was on first base. No one out, score tied. Jack Kramer, the Giants' pitcher, was at bat. Gil picked up their sign. He came to the mound and said, "Don't throw over."

Kramer squared to bunt. Hodges was charging hard as Kramer bunted down the first base line. Gil fielded it on one hop, tagged Kramer before he could get out of the batter's box, turned, and made a perfect catcher's throw to Jackie at second base to throw out the sliding Stanky. Score it 3 unassisted—a 3-4 double play.

Dr. Peale and Mr. Rickey

One of our frequent fans at Ebbets Field was Dr. Norman Vincent Peale, a friend of Branch Rickey's and several of us on the team. Dr. Peale used to enjoy talking about the Rickey commentary as the two of them sat in Mr. Rickey's private box.

On one occasion, a big, burly hitter came to the plate and hit a ground ball in the hole at shortstop. It was a very close play at first, and the batter was out by an eyelash.

Mr. Rickey jumped up and said, "Norman, Norman, did you see that? Did you see what just happened, Norman? There's a sermon in that!" Dr. Peale, somewhat bewildered, said, "What happened? What did I miss?" To which Mr. Rickey replied, "Norman, that big fellow, he was chewing tobacco. When he hit that ball, he took time to spit, then was out by a whisker. Norman, there's a sermon in that."

Dick Sisler

Baseball players are masters of the sharp needle. In fact, it's a big part of baseball to razz the opposing players. Most of the time it's taken in stride. If a player lets it bother him, he'll only get more.

One good-natured opponent was Dick Sisler of the Phillies. He was a good left-handed hitter, was always friendly, and had a good sense of humor. He did have a stuttering problem and took some kidding because of it. He had been a chief petty officer in the navy, so he was often greeted with "Whatta ya say, Ch-ch-ch-ch-Chief?" He'd always smile and say, "Fa-fa-fa-fa-fine, thanks."

We greeted him one day in the runway to the dugouts before game time, and he told us this story. He said he was standing in front of the Commodore Hotel, waiting for a cab to go to Ebbets Field, when a guy pulled up and said to him, "Hey, bu-bu-bu-bu-buddy, where's fo-fo-fo-fo-forty-second street?" Dick said, "I was af-af-af-af-afraid to answer."

Mel Queen

Mel Queen, a pitcher for Pittsburgh, arrived in the National League in 1948 and was not exactly known for his batting. Our bench would get on him each time he stepped to the plate, reminding him that he was no hitter. We could tell it was getting to him.

One day at Ebbets Field, Mel Queen hit a line drive over the second baseman for what was obviously a clean base hit. As he ran down the first base line, he was looking at our bench, giving us the big "ha, ha" because he finally had a base hit. To his surprise, Carl Furillo (aka the Reading Rifle), who was playing him shallow in right field, fielded the ball on one hop and threw him out at first base. Mel Queen had to return to his dugout past our bench.

Yankee Stadium

Many of my teammates and I were born in the 1920s, so we grew up when our national heroes were Babe Ruth and Lou Gehrig, two awesome players on some great Yankee teams. So when we played the first game of the 1949 World Series, it was the first time many of us had been in Yankee Stadium, "The House That Ruth Built." The Yankees had just remodeled the clubhouses and had moved the visitors' clubhouse to the third base side and relocated the Yankees behind first base.

I will always believe the Yankees deliberately intimidated a young Dodger team in a very calculated way. When we entered the visitors' locker room, we were not only confronted with the atmosphere of being in a national baseball shrine, but we also noticed that, still in place and not yet moved to the Yankees' side, were the lockers and uniforms of Babe Ruth and Lou Gehrig.

Yes, we lost the series, four games to one.

Joltin' Joe

It was the third game of the 1949 World Series at Ebbets Field. The Yankees had two men on base. The signal came from the bench to bring me in. I was in my second season, and this was my first World Series appearance. I didn't realize until I got to the mound and saw the hitter that I was to face Joe DiMaggio. What a moment! He hit a 400-foot drive—200 feet straight up over the shortstop, then 200 feet down—and Reese made the catch. Joe retired the next season, and I didn't face him again.

However, after I retired, Joe and I were together on several occasions. He represented the Bowery Savings Bank in New York, and I had become a banker in my hometown with First National Bank. When Bowery Savings opened offices in Brooklyn, I was invited to attend, along with Joe, and take part in the ribbon-cutting ceremony.

I did actually face Joe DiMaggio again in an Old-Timers' Game in Cleveland. He was in his 60s. I was still throwing a little batting practice for Anderson College, so when Joe came up, I wanted to throw him some good pitches to hit. The crowd wanted to see Joe hit one out. He fouled the first pitch, then the second, and third. Each time, he took that classic DiMaggio swing. A fourth foul, and then a fifth. The umpire tossed me another ball, and I was ready to throw another strike. Joe held up his left hand and said, "Hold it, Carl, let me get my breath."

My fantasy had come true—Joe DiMaggio asked me to ease up.

The Swami

During minor league days, spring training at Dodgertown in Vero Beach, Florida, was a captive experience, what with 200 or 300 minor leaguers battling for a place in pro baseball. The training camp was well out of town, and none of us had a car. At night there was lots of time to kill.

Chuck Connors used to do card tricks in the big lobby. One trick he did required the help of an accomplice. Chuck would send Toby Atwell down the road to a phone booth. Toby would sit in the booth with a flashlight and read a paperback Western and wait.

In the lobby, Connors would entice a few bets that he could have someone draw a card from the deck and then call the Swami, who would identify the card. For example, the ten of hearts is drawn; everybody in the room sees it. Connors then dials the number of the phone booth. Toby answers on the first ring and immediately begins to name the suits, "spades, hearts. . . ." Connors interrupts when he hears "hearts" by saying, "Hello, Swami." Toby then rapidly names the cards, "King, queen, jack, ten." Connors again interrupts on the "ten." Then he hands the phone to one of the bettors. In a monotone, Toby says, "This is the Swami. Your card is the ten of hearts," and hangs up. Connors picks up the money.

Happy

A. B. "Happy" Chandler was baseball's commissioner in the 1940s and early 1950s. He was formerly the govenor of Kentucky.

His nickname fit him perfectly because he was an outgoing, gregarious southern gentleman who never missed a chance to shake hands, slap your back, and ask, "How's Mama and the kiddies?"

Chandler, who is in the Hall of Fame, will best be known for his open support of Branch Rickey and the move to bring Jackie Robinson into professional baseball.

Chandler was also a wonderful storyteller. One tale he often told was about Honest John the umpire, always known for his knowledge of the rulebook and carrying it out to the letter.

Once, late in a game, a big farm boy on the visiting team hit the baseball so hard that the cover flew off. The rest of the ball rolled to the third baseman, who threw the runner out easily. However, Honest John called him safe, causing the home team to lose and creating a near riot.

When confronted with this obviously bad call, Honest John pulled out his rulebook and quoted from a section that read: "The opposing team must recover the ball before a putout can be made."

To Curve or Not to Curve?

One of the early TV shows in New York was *Omnibus*; it covered human interest stories and unusual events. The host was Burgess Meredith.

Omnibus contacted the Dodgers and asked if they would participate in a somewhat scientific study on whether a baseball really curves. They requested both a right-handed and a left-handed pitcher to be filmed throwing a curve. Preacher Roe and I were selected.

On the morning of the filming, Preacher and I went to Ebbets Field and dressed in full uniform. Several brand-new baseballs were provided. The balls had not been "rubbed up" as game balls always are, so they were slick and shiny. I was concerned that I might not be able to get the maximum curve break on the ball—I wanted to throw my best curve, my money pitch.

As we walked through the runway to the field, we passed a member of the grounds crew. I asked him if he had any fine sandpaper. He brought me a piece, and I lightly sanded the white leather, creating a "tiny fuzz" on the ball. Then I went to the mound and started loosening up.

The director came out and stood behind me as I threw to Art Dede, one of our scouts. The director admitted he wasn't much of a baseball man and said he wanted to check out what he had to film. By now I was warmed up, so the director said, "Throw a curve so I can take a look."

I fired an overhand curve. The ball must have curved three feet or more. It was the biggest curve I ever threw. "Oh, my God," the director exclaimed, "is there any doubt?"

When they aired the film on *Omnibus*, a straight white dotted line had been superimposed on the film to show the extent of the curve. It was convincing.

Once, Lefty Gomez, whose nickname was "Goofy," was asked if a curveball was just an optical illusion as some scientists had contended. Lefty, who was 6-0 in World Series play, said, "All I know is, I won a lot of games with my curveball, but when I lost my optical illusion, I had to quit."

Now You See It, Now You Don't

One of the feistiest players of the 1950s was a little infielder named Solly Hemus. Solly was a *brat*, one of those players who could scratch out a hit or a walk and find some way to beat you.

During a night game in St. Louis, Solly led off the ninth inning, score tied. On a high, tight pitch, Solly went down, but the ball caromed off of his bat, foul, above his head. However, Solly remained on the ground, rolling around, holding his thumb, and moaning as though he'd been hit. He rubbed his thumb enough that by the time Frank Secory, the home plate umpire, asked to look at it, sure enough, his thumb was noticeably red. Secory waved Hemus to first base. We argued and argued, but to no avail. Eventually in that inning, Hemus scored the run that beat us.

A couple of weeks passed, and we opened a series in Pittsburgh. Frank Secory happened to be back of the plate again. Our bench was on him from the first pitch and gave him a rough time each inning.

Late in the game, with the Pirates behind by one run, Pete Castiglione came to the plate with a man on first and no one out. Pete squared around to lay down a sacrifice bunt, but the pitch was well inside. Pete flinched, but the ball went "crack" and shot down the third base line, and the runner was an easy forceout at second.

Back at home plate, Castiglione was still in the batter's box, reeling as if in pain and holding his left wrist. He pleaded with Secory that he'd been hit by the pitch. Our bench really came alive and was heavy on Secory. Castiglione was denied first base, and he had to leave the game.

Two innings later, the field announcer informed the crowd that Castiglione's wrist was broken in two places. The old baseball adage is true: When you argue on a play, you're really arguing for the next close one.

Arthur Murray

Television was new in the late 1940s and early 1950s. There were numerous live TV shows coming out of New York: *The Ed Sullivan Show*, *Perry Como*, *What's My Line?* and a host of others. One of those popular shows was *The Arthur Murray Dance Party*. Arthur Murray and his wife, Kathryn, were known for their many dance studios located around the country. Their jingle was, "Arthur Murray teaches dancing in a hurry."

Duke Snider and I were contacted to appear on the show, along with Whitey Ford of the Yankees and Sal Maglie of the Giants. Arthur Murray told us beforehand that we would be participating in a dance contest. We could select any type of dance and be given a professional dancer as our partner. None of us was experienced at dancing, but Arthur assured us that our professional partner would make us look good. After a short rehearsal, Arthur Murray said, "Fellows, I want this to be hard competition—just like you guys go at it on the baseball field. To give you real incentive, I'm putting up $1,000 to the winner." Now that was big money! When Arthur left us for a few moments, Whitey said, "Look, let's split it $250 each way—no matter who wins." "Great!" we said.

Just minutes before showtime, Arthur Murray came back and said, "Don't forget, now—real strong competition. In fact, I'm going to double that prize money—$2,000 to the winner." Whitey winked and whispered, "Now it's $500 each." Whitey won the contest with his jitterbug partner, but we all shared the prize money.

Brooklyn Daze

There were certain players whose names were perfect for the Brooklyn tongue. In an earlier story, I mentioned that my own good name in Brooklynese was "Cal Oiskin." Two others were "Koiby" Higbe and "Dook" Snider.

Waite Hoyt was a star pitcher for the New York Yankees in the 1920s. The afternoon he was struck on the knee by a line drive, Yankee fans worried that it might be a career-ending injury. *The Brooklyn Eagle* carried a big black headline: "HOYT IS HURT." The Brooklyn baseball faithful were reading it, "HERT IS HOIT."

"Do As I Say, Not . . ."

Before Walt Alston became a Hall of Fame big-league manager, he was a schoolteacher in Oxford, Ohio, and a successful minor league manager.

When Walt managed the Dodgers' Triple A team in Montreal in 1950, I was sent there by the Dodgers to rehab my injured shoulder. On that team were pitchers Clyde King and Jack Banta. All three of us were starting pitchers, so to play golf together, we had to pick a day when none of us was pitching.

We had found only one day on this homestand when we could play golf. In the clubhouse meeting the night before our planned golf game, Walt Alston put a prohibition on any golf until the team started playing better. "Keep your mind on this game," he said.

Clyde, Jack, and I decided we'd go anyhow because it was our only chance. We got up at daylight and went to the golf course. While Clyde and Jack went into the pro shop, I was practicing on the putting green.

A taxi pulled up, and out stepped Lela and Walt Alston with their golf clubs. They had to walk right past me. They spoke and then continued to the first tee. We teed off right behind them and played 18 holes.

Walt never mentioned the incident. We always believed that he felt we had caught him the same way he had caught us.

The Five-Hitter

When Preacher Roe pitched, it was a clinic on control, change of speed, and, most important, how he psyched out the hitters. Preach had a reputation for throwing an illegal pitch: the spitball. In fact, he did have this unhittable pitch, but the way he didn't use it proved almost as effective as when he actually used it. Hitters were always expecting it, and Preacher was a master at deceiving them. These hitters would often call time and ask the umpire to look at the ball. On occasion, Preacher would act as though "you caught me this time," and instead of tossing the ball to the umpire, he would roll it in on the ground.

Preacher threw home runs frequently because he was always around the plate with his pitches and he hated to walk a batter. As a result, most of the homers hit off Preacher were with no one on base.

In a game against the Braves, Preacher had a two-hit, 5-0 lead going into the ninth inning. With one out, the next three consecutive pitches were hit for home runs. Preacher then retired the next two batters for a complete-game 5-3 win.

At Preacher's locker in the clubhouse, the writers were crowded around, all asking about the three consecutive home run pitches. Preach said, "Ah, fellas, come on. Just say Old Preacher pitched a complete game today and won. He scattered five hits. Two inside the park and three outside."

Elmer and Jocko

Elmer Sexauer was a minor league pitcher who was called up to the Dodgers in late season of 1950. Elmer had never even seen a major league game. He was thrilled beyond words to be in uniform and to see his first game.

The Dodgers were playing the Braves, and as the game began, our bench was already giving the plate umpire, Jocko Conlan, an earful. As the game progressed, so did the needling of Jocko. Then, on a close call at home plate, Jocko called our man out. Someone on our bench threw a white towel out of the dugout, which suggested that it was such a bad call that we give up. Umpires will take a lot, but they will not tolerate being shown up.

Jocko walked over to our bench, his Irish eyes flashing and his face skewed into a frown, and said to our manager, Burt Shotton, "OK, Burt, somebody has to go. Since I don't know who threw the towel, you pick him." Burt looked down our bench, deciding who he could best do without. Finally, he said, "The kid." Elmer was completely unaware of what was happening, so he just sat there. Jocko yelled, "You! Kid! You're outta here!" We finally had to tell Elmer he had been ejected. Quite bewildered, he picked up his glove and jacket and walked across Braves Field to the dugout runway. The Braves' fans were booing him severely as he left.

I've always wondered what Elmer wrote home to his folks about his first day in the big leagues.

Drop Dead

Gene Hermanski was a fun personality who always kept us loose on the bench. He also liked the horses and would spend his off days at the track. Once, he bet on his favorite horse at a New Jersey track. On the backstretch the horse had a heart attack. Gene was already having a bad day, so when he saw his horse collapse on the track, he moaned, "I bet on this horse to finish, and I lost."

Don Zimmer, also a track buff, called the racing form his "bible." As he left for the track, he usually said, "I hope I break even. I need the money."

A Hit's a Hit

The Brooklyn Dodger lineup was explosive and could score a lot of runs, and it did on September 1, 1950, against the Boston Braves. The final score was 19-3.

Gil Hodges had the biggest day, hitting four home runs. I always felt a special bond with Hodges because we were both from Indiana and had been scouted by the same Dodger scout, Stanley Feezle. Maybe that's why I had my biggest day at bat, getting four straight hits—not bad for a .150 hitter.

Each of Gil's blasts was crushed. Here's how mine went: The first was a sacrifice bunt that the Braves let roll, hoping it would go foul. It didn't, and I beat it out. The second hit was a broken-bat single over first base. The third was a bloop up the middle, barely far enough to reach the outfield grass. The fourth was a routine ground ball to Bob Elliot at third base. As Bob went down to field the ball, it hit a rock and sailed over his head.

All four of those hits laid end to end wouldn't have made one of Gil's homers. However, the next day in the box score, those four hits looked like four line drives.

"Gimme da Score"

The borough of Brooklyn was an orphan among the other boroughs of New York. Uptown Manhattan, the Bronx, and Harlem were the heart of New York City. Queens and Long Island were extensions of the biggest city in the world. But Brooklyn had few major theaters, hotels, or famous nightspots. It had no political clout, either; otherwise, the Dodgers might have remained in Brooklyn.

In addition, the baseball team had its troubles staying out of the second division. Tales were plentiful about bizarre happenings at Ebbets Field: outfielders getting hit on the head by fly balls, base runners running the wrong way, and fans who called their own team "Dem Bums."

Once, a cabbie pulled up in front of Ebbets Field during a game. An usher was standing outside, taking a break during the game, and the cabbie called, "How the Brooks doin'?" "They

Gil Hodges and I go four for four. (*Carl Erskine Collection*)

got three men on base," yelled the usher. The cabbie then asked, "Which base?"

A Line in the Sand

Al Barlick was a no-nonsense umpire. He was the most consistent umpire of his day, and he ran a tight ship. He was also a man of very few words. He once said, "On a close pitch, the hitter wants it, the pitcher wants it. I don't care who gets it." He spoke only when spoken to. He was definitely in charge of the game.

The leadoff hitter for the Braves was Johnny Logan. When Barlick called an inside pitch a strike, Johnny stepped out of the batter's box and, holding his bat by the barrel end, drew a line in the dirt some three or four inches inside, indicating where he thought the pitch was. Barlick, without a word, grabbed the bat and wrote, "$50 Fine" in the dirt. The game went on.

Mike Royko

The late Mike Royko was a popular and controversial columnist for the *Chicago Tribune* (and prior to that, the *Daily News* and the *Sun-Times*). He was street-smart and had lots of appeal because of his common sense and wit. He wrote mostly about Chicago and would take on anyone as fair game.

One of his favorite subjects was the Cubs. Because the team hadn't won a pennant since 1945, he had lots of ammunition. He also had a theory he called the "Cub Factor." He used a number of examples where two or more Cubs were traded to a contending team. Then, no matter how strong that team was, no matter how highly the oddsmakers rated the team, no matter how big a lead the team had, the "Cub Factor" would kick in, and that team would end up losing.

In 1951 the Dodgers played the Cubs at Wrigley Field in their first series of the season. In the clubhouse, Charlie Dressen called Gene Hermanski, Joe Hatten, Eddie Miksis, and Bruce Edwards up front. He told them to clear out their lockers and walk across the field to the Cubs' locker room. The four of them had just been traded.

In the meantime, over in the Cubs' clubhouse, four players—Wayne Terwilliger, Johnny Schmitz, Rube Walker, and Andy Pafko—were being told they had been traded to the Dodgers. It was a straight four-for-four deal; no money changed hands.

The players traded to the Dodgers were really strong, particularly with Pafko, who gave us that third strong outfielder to go with Duke Snider and Carl Furillo. We sailed through the first half of the season. By August the Dodgers had a 13 1/2-game lead. The Giants would gain a game or two, but we still had a big cushion. The Giants kept coming. In an unbelievable finish, the Giants tied the Dodgers on the final day of the season. That forced a best-of-three playoff. The Giants won the first game; the Dodgers won the second. Then, in Game 3, Bobby Thomson hit the "Shot heard 'round the world"—a three-run homer in the bottom of the ninth to win the pennant. Ralph Branca, the pitcher who threw the gopher ball, has been blamed. Charlie Dressen has been blamed. Clyde Sukeforth, the coach who picked Branca, has been blamed. Mike Royko had the answer all along: "The Cub Factor."

The Truth

The Giants-Dodgers series of the 1950s were electrifying, intense, and hard-fought. Leo Durocher and Charlie Dressen had the same philosophy about knockdown pitches. "Give 'em two for one." Of course, that's the type of thinking that keeps wars going.

A master of the knockdown pitch was the Giants' Sal "The Barber" Maglie, who could have shaved the back of your neck just below your cap. His favorite targets among the Dodgers were Jackie Robinson, Roy Campanella, and Carl Furillo. When Maglie pitched, we knew somebody was going down.

At a night game in Ebbets Field, I hooked up with "The Barber." Sure enough, he threw his purpose pitch, once to Roy, then to Jackie. When I came to bat, Sal threw me a fastball that was riding high inside and coming directly at me. I froze, and the ball banged inside and shot down the third base line—foul. Jackie was off the bench and at the plate in a flash. "It hit him, the ball hit him," he screamed at umpire Jocko Conlan. I just stood there in shock. Jackie kept yelling at Jocko, "The ball hit him." (Jocko, a no-nonsense umpire, was accidentally kicked in the shin once by Durocher, who was kicking dirt on the plate, but Jocko didn't throw Leo out or fine him. He just kicked him back in the shin with his steel-toed umpire's shoe.) So he said to Jackie, "I couldn't tell whether the ball hit him or not." Jocko turned to me and asked, "Did that ball hit you?" I was still shook up and just honestly replied, "No, Jocko, it hit the knob of the bat."

Jackie's mouth dropped open in disbelief. He looked like he had been betrayed. I was too stunned to say anything but the truth.

Janice

In my 1945 high school graduating class was a talented and beautiful girl named Janice McArt. I signed into pro baseball the next year, and Janice pursued show business as a singer and performer. By the 1950s, we had both made the big leagues; I was with the Brooklyn Dodgers, and she was on Broadway.

The Dodgers were returning from a long road trip and had landed at LaGuardia Airport. As we walked through the terminal at LaGuardia in a group of about 40—including players, writers, managers, and coaches—almost in unison we saw this gorgeous-looking gal coming toward us—pink flowery dress, big floppy hat, and a fur piece—high-stepping it and coming right our way. Following her was a chauffeur in full uniform carrying her several pieces of luggage. As she got closer, I saw that it was Janice McArt. We had heard about each other's success, but hadn't seen each other since our school days in Anderson, Indiana. When she spotted me, she let out a loud scream, raced over to me, threw her arms around me, and said, "Oh, Carl, you look wonderful. I'm rushing to catch a plane but, honey, I'll try to see you when I get back." Swoosh! She was gone.

Forty guys stopped in their tracks, all looking at me. Finally, Chuck Dressen, our little firebrand manager, said in a loud voice, "See, I told you guys you gotta watch them guys that drink only milkshakes!"

Pickoff

One of my best memories of our captain, Pee Wee Reese, was how he helped me win some games with a pickoff play at second base.

The Dodgers were a good teaching organization, and the pitchers were taught how to become the fifth infielder on bunts, covering first and making throws to the bases. Most pitchers, however, were gun-shy when it came to pickoff attempts at second base. If the throw was errant, the runner would advance and possibly even score, so it was chancy to throw to second.

Pee Wee encouraged me to wheel and throw back to second once he gave me the pickoff sign. He insisted that I turn from my set position on the mound and throw hard, directly toward second base. One of three things would happen: (1) we would pick the runner off; (2) the runner would get back to the bag and the ball would drill him in the back; or (3) if the throw missed its mark, it still had enough velocity that the center fielder would be able to retrieve the ball in time to hold the runner at second.

Once, against the Braves, I was working with the bases loaded in the ninth inning, two outs, and a 3-2 count on Earl Torgeson. The whole ballgame was riding on this next payoff pitch. To my surprise, Pee Wee gave me the pickoff sign. I came set, wheeled, and threw a strike to Pee Wee and picked off Sibby Sisti to end the game. Torgeson, in the batter's box, was so upset that he broke his bat, slamming it on home plate. Thanks to Pee Wee, I never had to make that critical pitch.

Bed Check

Managers have the difficult job of being father, police officer, teacher, pastor, psychologist, and taskmaster, all at the same time. Casey Stengel was quoted as saying, "The toughest job for a manager is to keep the guys who hate you away from the guys who are undecided."

Most managers have curfews, bed checks, and other basic rules to keep 25 hot-blooded, sometimes hot-headed, players under control—especially on road trips.

Charlie Dressen was very perceptive and often picked up on a player's behavior without even trying. Once, he saw rookie pitcher Johnny Podres sitting in a bar. He told him that wasn't the place for him to be. Johnny said, "I was just here for a 7-Up." Charlie said, "Next time, have it at a soda fountain—then there's no question."

Charlie had lots of friends all over the league and often came in very late at night. (Of course, he didn't have to honor his 1:00 a.m. curfew.) One time, he returned to the hotel in Chicago after a night out, about 3:00 a.m. As he entered the elevator, the young man who was operating the elevator said, "You know, Mr. Dressen, you have some great young men playing for you. See this baseball? I took three of your players up to the sixth floor just minutes ago. They all signed this baseball." Charlie looked at the three names, and the next day he fined them $100 each.

The Mike

The fan in the stands sees all the action on the field but has to speculate about what is being said when there's a conference on the mound or at home plate.

Once, the New York Giants decided to bury a microphone at home plate to hear the umpires go over the ground rules and the managers exchange lineup cards. Great idea, right?

It only lasted two innings. In the third inning, Leo Durocher, the Giants' manager, charged the home plate umpire on a close call that went against the Giants. In his eloquent style of profanity, he scorched the umpire and sent some smoking sound waves over radio and TV and through the PA system. Thanks to that outburst, to this day, fans still have to guess what is being said on the field.

For the record, during a mound conference, the pitcher might hear this kind of instruction from his manager: "Now look, the tying run is on third base and the winning run is at the plate. He's the league-leading hitter. Don't give him anything good to hit, but don't walk him."

Willie the Wonder

It has been said that Babe Ruth never threw to the wrong base or made any other mental errors—that he had great baseball instincts. Willie Mays fits that description. He came into the big leagues and made all of the plays properly from day one. Many of his great defensive plays were unique— it was obvious that he could never have actually practiced them.

One such play happened at the Polo Grounds. Billy Cox of the Dodgers was on third base with one out. Carl Furillo hit a screaming line drive deep to right center field. It looked like a certain extra-base hit. Cox tagged up at third, just to be sure. Willie, sprinting over from center field, took a headlong dive with outstretched arm and glove and made an unbelievable catch. That, however, was only the front end of the greatest catch and throw imaginable.

Willie hit the ground and instinctively rolled, getting back on his feet, and in the same motion threw blindly toward home plate, some 350 feet away. His throw was a perfect strike on the low third base side of home plate. Cox, who had tagged, was such an easy out that he didn't even bother sliding. He just stared in disbelief as Wes Westrum tagged him to complete the astounding double play.

Willie made so many great catches that he was often asked which one was his best. Willie's honest answer was, "I just catch 'em; I don't compare 'em."

Babe's Watch

The Brooklyn Dodgers had a very rowdy bench. We had to be good, because we usually made everybody mad before the game ever started. Leo Durocher, who at the time was managing the Giants, was a great target for at least two of our players, Jackie Robinson and Don Newcombe. Of course, Leo was a master at superlatives and eloquent profanity, so there were some classic exchanges.

During Leo's playing days as a fancy-fielding Yankee shortstop, his teammate Babe Ruth had a watch missing from his locker. Rumor had it that Leo was the thief. Actually, it was never known what happened to the watch, but what ammunition for Big Newk. As soon as Leo would appear on the field or in the Giant dugout, Newk would get the day started with his big, booming voice: "Hey, Leo, go see what time it is on Babe Ruth's watch." Then the fun began!

Famous Pitch

Sometimes becoming famous carries with it a big price tag. Ralph Branca, an outstanding Dodger pitcher, gained some of his fame early in his career. In 1947, at age 21, he won 21 games. Ralph had other winning seasons also; however, his name is more famous in baseball history for just one pitch he threw.

In 1951 the New York Giants pulled a miracle finish to catch and tie the Dodgers after being 13 1/2 games behind in August. This tie on the final day of the season forced a best-of-three playoff series to decide the National League pennant.

The Giants won Game 1. The Dodgers won Game 2 when Clem Labine hurled a 10-0 shutout. Newcombe had the start for Game 3 and took a two-run lead into the ninth inning. Two "seeing eye" base hits brought the potential winning run to home plate in the person of Bobby Thomson. Charlie Dressen called the bullpen at the Polo Grounds, where Branca and I were warming up. Clyde Sukeforth answered the phone. "They're both ready," he said. "However, Erskine is bouncing his overhand curve." Dressen said, "Let me have Branca." On

Ralph's second pitch, Thomson hit a three-run homer to win the game and the pennant.

Whenever I'm asked what my best pitch was, I say, "The curveball I bounced in the Polo Grounds bullpen."

Good Faith

W ho is most important to the game of baseball: the owner of the team, the talented players, or the supportive fans? The obvious answer is that all three are necessary—especially the fans.

The tug-of-war between labor and management carried over onto the baseball scene. In 1966, the major league players decided to hire Marvin Miller to head the Major League Players Association (MLPA), which had been fairly ineffective since its inception in 1953.

Before that time, teams did have a player representative who would meet with owners to discuss various player concerns. One of the major agreements between owners and players was a handshake agreement on sharing the newfound revenue from television rights to air the All-Star Game and the World Series. A.B. "Happy" Chandler, commissioner of baseball, negotiated the very first contract with the networks in 1950. It was for $6 million dollars for five years, or $1.2 million per year.

The owners agreed to a 60/40 split, allowing 60 percent to help secure a creditable players' pension plan. J. Norman Lewis was counsel for the players and was instrumental in guiding us in negotiations. Allie Reynolds and Ralph Kiner represented the players.

In the decades since, TV revenue has skyrocketed. In the 1990s, the contract went for more than $1 billion! The players now enjoy one of the best pensions of any profession. Current players have continued to look back and upgrade older players' pensions.

J. Norman Lewis encouraged us as player reps to organize. "Now is the time," he said. Kiner and Reynolds, speaking for the players, said no. We had negotiated with the owners in good faith and accomplished our mission. In our day, the only strike we recognized was the one that Al Barlick or Jocko Conlan called.

The Redheads

Walter "Red" Barber was the voice of the Dodgers for many years and set a new standard of professionalism in sports broadcasting. Because his early years were before television, he used radio to send strong images through his broadcasts. One of his unique techniques was to remain silent for an unusually long time after a big hit or a home run, allowing the mike to be flooded with crowd noises. If you were listening on radio, that took you right into the ballpark. He was also skilled at reading a ticker tape and re-creating the game without actually seeing it.

In order to be sure he gave the score often enough to keep the fans updated about the game, Red used a regular kitchen egg timer in the booth. It took three minutes for the sand to run through the glass tube, so Red would give the score and then turn the timer over to run through again. He gave the score at least every three minutes.

Redheaded Vin Scully, fresh out of Fordham University, joined Barber in the booth in 1952. Vin learned well. He was the voice of the Dodgers for more than 50 years.

Two famous redheads: legendary broadcasters Red Barber and Vin Scully. *(Courtesy of the Dodgers)*

TALES FROM THE DODGERS DUGOUT

Highs and Loes

Billy Loes, a young right-handed pitcher, was one of many strong arms developed in the Dodgers' deep minor league system. His fastball was exceptionally "live" and had great movement.

Billy was rather eccentric, and that's the polite way of putting it. "Squirrelly" was what most of his teammates called him. He was very superstitious and did some peculiar things to prevent bad luck. At team meetings before a game in which he was the starting pitcher, he would sit in front of his locker, which was behind a huge pillar, while the manager and the team sat in the open meeting space on the other side. Although he was completely out of sight, he would go over the opposing team's lineup and discuss how he would pitch to each batter. We could hear his voice but not see him.

Ticket

I once got a traffic ticket in Brooklyn, and after receiving a couple of warnings in the mail, I went down to the courthouse on Saturday morning before a day game to pay my fine.

I was standing in a long line of people, and the line was moving very slowly. In a while, a man came up to me and said with a sort of surprised expression, "Aren't you Cal Oiskin of the Dodgers?" I said I was. "What are you doing in this line?" he said. "Well, I got this ticket. I'm here to pay it." "Come on," he said, "follow me. I'll take you back to the judge's chambers before he goes on the bench. You don't have to wait in that long line." So I followed him into the judge's chambers. For the next half hour I listened to the judge. He told me all about his playing days in baseball and showed me his crooked fingers from catching in amateur baseball. Then he said, "Boy, am I glad to see you, a different Dodger. Gil Hodges is a regular down here." I got off for five bucks!

Smooth

When night baseball was introduced in Brooklyn, the general manager, Larry MacPhail, had some new ideas about baseball under the lights. First he tried an orange-colored ball and then a yellow one. Neither proved to be appropriate.

Then he had satin uniforms made to magnify the brilliant white and Dodger blue under the lights. They did look great, reflecting the lights, but they were miserable to play in.

Ballplayers must, I mean, must, do three things: spit, scratch, and wipe their hands on their pants or shirt. Wiping your hands was impossible with satin. It was so slick that your hand would just slide off. Anywhere you touched was the same. It was frustrating.

Thankfully, these uniforms were used only in spring training for the coaches. The photograph on the next page shows John Corriden and Andy High (in the satin uniforms) coaching Dick Williams, who is in a light wool uniform.

Rocky

Rocky Bridges, a journeyman infielder, came up through the Dodger farm system. Rocky was a humorist, and he maintained his good nature even though he didn't play a lot of innings.

Often Rocky would post a list in the clubhouse of his "All-Ugly" major league lineup. He also carried a spoon handle in

John Corriden and Andy High give some pointers to Dick Williams. *(Carl Erskine Collection)*

his pocket, and when he ordered a cup of black coffee, he'd slip the spoon handle in his cup. Then, calling the waitress over, he would say, "This coffee looks real strong." The waitress would look closely at it as Rocky would stir, then pull out the spoon with no end.

Once, during the Korean War, Rocky was ordered to go for his physical and possible army induction. He was really anxious. When he came back from his physical, he said, "I've got a heart murmur. It keeps murmuring, 'I don't want to go, I don't want to go.'" He didn't go.

Dry Side

Preacher Roe had an outstanding pitching career. He revealed, after retiring, that during his last few years, he had need of a new pitch. Harry Brecheen, his hunting buddy in Arkansas and a class pitcher for the Cardinals, showed him how to throw a spitball. Preacher said it kept him around long enough to make an additional $100,000. When Dick Young of the *Daily News* wrote about this for *Sports Illustrated* magazine, he titled it "You Can't Spit on $100,000." (Preacher later told me that he regretted revealing that he threw a spitter because he felt it hurt his chances to get into the Hall of Fame.)

One day in Ebbets Field, facing Stan Musial in a win-or-lose situation, Preach threw him what he called his "Beechnut Sinker," referring to the only chewing gum that gave him the right stuff. Musial doubled off the right field wall to beat the Preach. Next day, Preacher waited for Stan in the runway to the dugouts. "How'd you hit my best pitch?" Preacher asked him. Stan said, "I knew I'd get that wet one, and I always hit that kind on the dry side."

An Insult

Many of my most lasting and vivid memories of my 14 years in professional baseball come from the nine seasons I got to play with Jackie Robinson. This intelligent, polished, well educated man was a great motivator of the Brooklyn Dodgers from 1947 through 1956. The franchise, which had seldom won a National League pennant, captured six during his career and its one and only World Series championship in 1955.

"Intense," "competitive," "driven," and "on fire" describe only in part the wholeness and wholesomeness of this sharecropper's son. Biographers, historians, and sportswriters have missed some of the broader dimensions of this remarkable individual.

Jackie believed in self-help. Do it yourself; don't wait for someone, a change in law, or good luck to raise you above and out of a low set of circumstances or low self-esteem. He lived this philosophy, and the Jackie Robinson Foundation, governed by his capable wife, Rachel, still follows this same philosophy today. Self-control and self-determination were the hallmarks of his life.

Was he human? Oh yes. Take, for example, an incident in Cincinnati on a Sunday during a July doubleheader.

Excursion trains from the South—Atlanta, Birmingham, and other southern cities—would pour into the historic terminal in Cincinnati just to see Jackie. Crosley Field was packed. The temperature was in the high 90s.

We had finished the first game and the second was about to start when a black fan came down the aisle toward the dugout where Jackie was standing. This fan had had his fair share of beer. He was pretty unstable, and although he was dressed to the hilt when the day began, he now looked very disheveled, sloppy, and in total disarray. Jackie watched him.

"I wanna see Jackie," the fan slurred in a loud voice. "Where's my boy Jackie?"

By now he had reached the rail by the dugout. Jackie was so offended that he responded, "Why you sloppy, drunken, no-account . . . get out of my sight. Go home and clean up. I'll bet your front yard looks just like you do."

Jackie was indignant. The fan's state was an affront to all he stood for. After the outburst, the fan disappeared into the crowd.

Batter Up

The many humorous stories about Yogi Berra relate to his own way of seeing things.

At one point in Yogi's career, he was breaking a lot of bats. When Frank Ryan, the representative of Hillerich & Bradsby, maker of the Louisville Slugger, visited the Yankees on his regular rounds of the teams, Yogi complained that his own bats had "bad wood" in them. The rep told Yogi to save a couple of his broken bats so he could examine them. When Yogi showed him some of the broken bats, it was obvious why they were breaking. The bat was being held wrong, and the ball was striking the bat against the grain instead of with the grain. Yogi insisted that he always held the trademark up, which is correct. However, when the rep watched him swing, Yogi was rolling his wrists and actually contacting the ball on the wrong side. When the rep discussed his observations with Yogi and told him to hold the trademark on the back side instead of up, Yogi said, "Oh no. You guys in Louisville need to stamp that trademark on the wrong side so it's right when I swing. I always hold the trademark up." From then on, the famous bat maker burned its famous logo into the wrong side of Yogi's bats.

The Bridge Game

The baseball clubhouse is a kind of sanctuary for the players, and much of what happens there is not made public. On certain occasions, however, some interesting events take place there that do make the papers.

One such incident took place on June 19, 1952. The Chicago Cubs played the Brooklyn Dodgers in an afternoon game at Ebbets Field. It was a heavy, overcast day, and rain was almost certain. As I sat in the dugout just minutes before warming up as the starting pitcher, Vin Scully, the young broadcaster, walked over and sat down by me. I was holding the warmup baseball, and I said to Vin, "I wonder what the little pill has in store for me today." Vin often recalls that incident in his broadcasts.

The game started under ominous skies. The Dodgers scored quickly off of Warren Hacker, and he was replaced by Willy "The Knuck" Ramsdell. My job now was to get the Cubs out as quickly as possible and complete five innings before the rains came so that it would be an official game. When Ramsdell, a notoriously weak hitter, came to the plate in the third inning, I walked him on four straight pitches. The rains came, and we all rushed into the clubhouse. It poured and poured.

It was standard procedure for the Dodger team to play cards during such delays. We began a bridge game around one of the big uniform trunks. We played for 40 minutes, and I had just made a four-heart hand when the word came that the rain had stopped and the game would continue. I hurriedly changed into a dry uniform, warmed up again, and completed the nine-inning victory, 5-0. It turned out to be a no-hitter as well as a shutout, and Ramsdell was the only Cub to reach base, making him the "Star of the Game" on Happy Felton's postgame show.

The next day I got a phone call in the clubhouse. It was Charles Goren, the bridge expert, who had read about the bridge game during the rain delay. He wanted me to re-create my bridge hand.

Although I could recall with certainty every pitch I threw that day, I could not remember my bridge hand. Goren created one himself to tell the story in his column.

Happy Felton

One of the famous nonplaying personalities at Ebbets Field was Happy Felton. He had a popular postgame television show that originated from the ballpark called *Talk to the Stars*. Each game he would pick one player from each team as "Star of the Game" and have both of them appear live on his show, answering phone calls from fans. This appearance on Happy's show also amounted to an extra payday, because if you made the show, you received $50.

On June 19, 1952, I started against the Cubs at Ebbets Field. In the ninth inning, Happy Felton sent his assistant, Larry McDonald, to the Cubs dugout to catch Willie Ramsdell as the possible "Star of the Game." Through eight innings, Willie had been the only Cub base runner. As Happy would tell me later, Willie sat in the TV room under the stands watching the Cubs bat in the top of the ninth. Willie was pulling for me to get the side out. With two outs, Eddie Miksis was the Cub batter. If he got a hit to break up the no-hitter, Willie would be out as the star of the game. Happy said Willie was talking to Miksis through the TV screen: "If you get a hit, you louse, I'll kill ya." Miksis grounded out to end the game. Willie was the Cubs' "Star of the Game" and got his 50 bucks.

First Aid

Clyde King was a studious and talented right-handed pitcher. He was used a lot in relief and was effective because of his good control and knowledge of the hitters. He was also alert to hitters' mannerisms, and if he caught a batter casually looking down, adjusting his feet in the batter's box, Clyde would quick-pitch him while he wasn't looking.

Once, Clyde was called into a game before he had time to get fully warmed up. When he told Charlie Dressen that he needed more pitches, Charlie gave Pee Wee Reese the sign to stall awhile and give Clyde a chance to throw a few more warmup pitches.

Pee Wee faked that he had something in his eye. Clyde happened to look back at shortstop and saw Pee Wee seemingly having trouble, so he quit throwing, left the mound, took out his handkerchief, and went to Pee Wee's aid.

The Ride

My dad was in all his glory at World Series time, when the Brooklyn Dodgers and New York Yankees were involved in a subway series.

When the games were in Yankee Stadium, the Dodgers provided two luxury buses—one for the team and one for the families. For my dad, the games took second place to the bus ride. We would leave Ebbets Field to the cheers and hoopla of Dodger fans lining the streets as we passed. The police escort, with sirens blaring, announced to the world, "Here come the Dodgers."

Soon we crossed the Brooklyn Bridge into lower Manhattan. The crowds thinned out a bit and were quite orderly, with fans just waving and smiling. Then we entered the Bronx—Yankee land. Now came the jeers, insulting signs, and a barrage of tomatoes, toilet paper, and eggs splattering the buses. My dad always had a seat right behind the driver so he could watch it all. The return trip held more of the same.

We all knew what the Yankee buses were in for when the games moved to Ebbets Field. The war zone started when the Yankees crossed the Brooklyn Bridge.

Billy Loes

Billy Loes, a talented right-handed pitcher, is second only to Yogi Berra in well remembered but puzzling quotes. As the Dodgers entered the 1952 World Series, writers were asking our players their predictions for the Series. Reese said Dodgers in six, Hodges said Dodgers in seven, and so on, until Loes was asked. He said, "If it goes to seven, I've got to pick the Yankees." He was right. That's the Series in which Loes is remembered for having missed a ground ball. He said the sun got in his eyes.

Gomez

As a minor-leaguer, I played a season of winter baseball in Havana, Cuba. My manager was Lefty Gomez, a great Yankee pitcher of the Babe Ruth era and a Hall of Famer. He was also known for his quick wit.

A few years later, I was in the big leagues, and Lefty was working for Wilson Sporting Goods and often showed up as he visited major league clubs to sell uniforms and other equipment.

The Dodgers were working out at Yankee Stadium the day before the 1952 World Series opener. I had just finished throwing batting practice and went over to the dugout to get a

Manager Charlie Dressen hangs out with his pitchers—me, Preacher Roe, Billy Loes, and Russ Meyer. *(Carl Erskine Collection)*

drink. Lefty had come in to watch the workout and was sitting there in the dugout. We greeted each other with the usual amiable exchanges. "How's Betty?" he asked me, "and your kids?" "Real fine," I said. "How about June and your family?" He gave me the rundown on his family and then added, "Of course, the baby just turned six months old and is doing great."

Just then, Jack Lang, a New York sportswriter who traveled with us, happened to step into the dugout. He said, "Lefty, did I hear you say you have a baby six months old at your age?" Quick as his once good fastball, Lefty said, "That was my arm that went dead."

Last Resort

There are times when a pitcher just can't find a way to get certain hitters out. In that frustrating situation, a pitcher will resort to almost anything—legal or illegal. Often the inclination is to throw harder, but Preacher Roe took a different approach.

Preacher's nemesis was big Walker Cooper. Although they were friends off the field, the meeting turned vicious when Cooper had a bat in his hand. After having no luck with his fastball, slider, and curveball, Preacher came up with what he hoped would be an "in your face" delivery that Walker couldn't hit.

Preacher would take a very slow windup and then take an exceptionally long stride. When his extended foot would hit the ground, Preacher would hold that position, hesitating a couple of seconds and then throw a high looping curve. It would float toward the plate in a high arc, coming down in Cooper's face.

Preacher called it his "go to hell" pitch. Cooper would watch this slow ball descend and then spit at it as it went by. It turned out that was the surest way to hit it.

What Goes Around Comes Around

The saying "What goes around comes around" has many applications in baseball. One of those that I experienced took place with an outstanding pitcher, Johnny Sain. He was a standout with the Boston Braves, along with Warren Spahn. Their pitching rotation was "Spahn and Sain, then pray for rain." Johnny won a World Series game, beating Bob Feller 1-0 in the first game of the 1948 World Series. The winning run for Boston was scored by Phil Masi after a controversial call by umpire Bill Stewart. Masi had clearly been picked off second base by Feller, as Lou Boudreau put the tag on Masi. Bill Stewart, however, called Masi safe. He then scored on a base hit by Tommy Holmes to make Sain the lucky winning pitcher. Feller was the unlucky loser.

In the 1952 World Series, fifth game against the Yankees, I gave up five runs in the fifth inning. Manager Charlie Dressen surprised the world by leaving me in the game. The game went 11 innings, and we won, 6-5. From the fifth inning to the 11th inning, I did not allow another Yankee base runner—19 consecutive outs. However, right in the middle of that string, Johnny Sain, who was in relief of Ewell Blackwell, hit a ground ball back of second base. Jackie Robinson made a great stop and throw. Art Passarella, the first base umpire, called Sain out. Bill Dickey, coaching first, and Sain argued fiercely, but the out stood. Pictures in the papers the next day showed that Sain was clearly safe at first base.

Johnny Sain was waiting for me the next day and gave me a real chewing out for getting such an undeserved win. He was really worked up over that call. After enduring his sour grapes for several minutes, I said, "Johnny, who got the win in the 1948 World Series when Masi was picked off second base?" What goes around comes around.

[Editor's note: Interestingly, it wasn't until later that Carl Erskine learned that his nine nonconsecutive no-hit, no-run innings were only one inning shy of Babe Ruth's World Series record of 10 nonconsecutive no-hit, no-run innings in a 14-inning game, set in 1918 against—who else?—the Dodgers. Of course, four years later, the Yankees' Don Larsen pitched the first and only perfect Series game . . . alas, against the Dodgers.]

Fives Alive

I was the starting pitcher for Game 5 of the World Series in 1952. When I arrived at my locker in Yankee Stadium, there were several telegrams from friends and fans wishing me good luck. One in particular from a fan in Texas said, "Good luck in the fifth game of the World Series, on this fifth day of October, and congratulations on your fifth wedding anniversary." This all happened to be true; I just hadn't thought about it.

Red Barber, our announcer, was strolling along the lockers, chatting with Dodger players, and when he got to me, I showed him this telegram. He said, "That's fascinating. May I take it to the booth? It may come in handy." His announcing partner was a very young Vin Scully.

I totally forgot about the telegram and went on with my pregame routine. After four innings, we were leading, 4-0. Then came the fifth. The Yankees scored five runs in the fifth. The big blow was a three-run homer by Johnny Mize. Charlie Dressen came to the mound, talked with me, and then to everyone's surprise, left me in the game. I got Yogi Berra out to end the inning. We tied the game in the seventh and won it on a Duke Snider double in the 11th. In the bottom of the 11th, Berra took a third strike to end the game. Vin Scully said the fives became so significant that he was watching intently for any other five connection. He swears that he looked at the stadium clock as the game ended—five minutes past five.

Betty and the Boys

The fans watching from the stands only see a part of what's happening on the field. For instance, when a pitcher faces a hitter he has faced dozens of times over several years, both hitter and pitcher know each other's strengths and weaknesses. So it becomes an invisible mind game. This game is really more important than what the fans see. The fan only sees the results.

Signs and signals are happening constantly, and hand signals from the bench continuously fine-tune the defensive positions of the fielders. I'm sure the fans watching me pitch saw a pretty standard routine of wind-up, throw, field my position, etc. However, what the fans didn't see was one of my greatest moments of true joy.

As I stood on the mound looking at Campy, my catcher, for the next sign, the fans couldn't know I was actually looking right past him into the stands, where, in about the second inning, Betty would be coming down the aisle to the box behind home plate reserved for players' families. With her were my two little boys, Danny and Gary—all three of them polished and beautiful. I would watch them and say to myself, "Look at you, you lucky guy—pitching in the big leagues for a great team on a beautiful day in a great ballpark and privileged to have that wonderful family." Fully inspired, I would then look at Campy for the next sign and go on with my day's work.

Betty and sons Danny and Gary greet me at New York's
LaGuardia Airport after a road trip. *(Carl Erskine Collection)*

Signs of the Times

Some people believe that baseball is too slow with not much happening between pitches. They think ballplayers spit and scratch more than they actually play the game. But that's a dead giveaway that the game is more complex than people think.

For instance, during the time between pitches, signs are constantly being relayed—from catcher to pitcher, infield to outfield, and bench to bullpen. In my time it was all hand signals; there were no phones at Ebbets Field in my early seasons.

When manager Charlie Dressen wanted a certain pitcher to start throwing in the bullpen, he had to step out of the dugout, look down the right field foul line, and signal our bullpen. If he wanted our big Italian right-hander Ralph Branca, he would bend forward and mimic eating stringy spaghetti. If he wanted sinkerballer Ed Roebuck, he would pretend he was rowing a boat. If he wanted me—Erskine—he would pull on his right ear and then touch his skin (ear-skin). These were signs that were never missed.

Tricks of the Trade

Every profession has its inside strategies that help a person gain an advantage. For a sinkerball pitcher, the grounds crew may wet down the area in front of home plate so that the hard-hit ground balls will lose some zip. And because the mounds are reshaped after every game, often the grounds crew will customize it for the home team's next starting pitcher, making it steeper for an overhand pitcher or flatter for a side-armer.

When a relief pitcher enters the game, he usually does some housekeeping on the mound. In the process, he may cover up the pitching rubber, then pitch eight to 10 inches in front of it. Another slick trick is for the pitcher to get ready to deliver, watch for the hitter to look down to adjust his stance, and then quick-pitch him. This is legal, unless time has been called.

Batters have their own defenses. A hitter may rub out the back line of the batter's box in order to stand deeper as he faces a hard-throwing pitcher; or he may rub out the front line so he can stand closer to hit a curveball pitcher before the curve breaks.

A seasoned catcher can distract a rookie batter by carrying on a conversation with him while the pitcher is winding up. Some catchers may even grab a handful of dirt and slowly sift it into the shoe of the hitter as the pitch is on its way.

Before 1950, it was customary for the infielders to leave their gloves on the grass behind their position between innings. The opposing infielders would sometimes take their wad of chewing tobacco and stuff it up a finger of the nearest glove. Next inning, you could see that infielder work all inning trying to dig it out between pitches.

Stealing signs from the catcher is an art form unto itself. One technique is to station a "spy" with binoculars in a concealed spot in the center field scoreboard. The catcher's sign is relayed by phone to the bench, and a word sign is then yelled to the batter. It was always suspected (mostly by Dodger players and fans) that the Giants in the Polo Grounds used this technique—especially before Bobby Thomson's "shot heard 'round the world," his playoff home run that sank the Dodgers in 1951 and gave the Giants the NL pennant. In an article in the *Wall Street Journal* some Giants players admitted to having a buzzer system to steal and relay signals.

However, knowing what's coming isn't always the advantage it might seem. When Orlando Cepeda came into the league, Braves pitcher Lew Burdette couldn't get him out. Cepeda hit everything Burdette threw. Finally, Burdette told his catcher, Del Crandall, to tell Cepeda what pitch was coming—

even the location. After that, Burdette started getting Cepeda out regularly.

Playing Hardball

When Buzzie Bavasi signed pitcher Billy Loes to his 1953 contract, it was only after a tough negotiation. Loes balked at $13,000 for the year, but Buzzie said, "Look, Bill, you won 13 games last year—that's a thousand dollars a win." So Loes signed.

Later that season, Loes beat the Cardinals in late August and went straight to our traveling secretary, Lee Scott, and asked for a ticket back to New York. Lee said, "Billy, we go to Chicago and Cincinnati before we go home." "No," said Loes, "I'm going home now. I'm getting paid to win 13 games. I just did it. Get me a ticket home."

Actually Billy stayed and even won another game that year, finishing 14-8. He still complained that he was underpaid.

Cimoli Squeeze

Billy Herman was convinced that he had a great system for giving signs. Our suicide squeeze play involved three signs. Billy, coaching at third base, would give the squeeze sign to the batter. The batter would then signal back to Billy that he got the sign. A word sign would then be given to the base runner, whose mission was to sprint home on the very next pitch. The word sign was the runner's last name.

We were trailing the Pirates by five runs. Gino Cimoli was on first when Duke Snider singled to right. Cimoli came sliding into third base and was safe—just beating the throw. The photographers were on the field in those days, and one of them

was squatting down behind the coaching box, taking a shot of
the sliding Cimoli. As Cimoli was dusting himself off, the photographer was making notes of the play and asked Billy Herman
who the runner was. Billy said, "Cimoli." The photographer,
who apparently didn't hear Billy clearly, said, "Who?" So, much
louder, Billy said, "Cimoli!" Gino's ears went up, and he took
off on the next pitch and was out by a mile.

We lost the game, and in the clubhouse, Billy was screaming at Cimoli. Cimoli just kept saying, "What's the squeeze
sign, Billy?"

Barney

I t's often been suggested that if you don't want to work all
of your life, find something you enjoy so much that it's not
like having a job.

Barney Stein was one of our club photographers, and he
loved his job. Among several award-winning photos, he took
was one of first baseman Gil Hodges, emphasizing Gil's great
hands. In that photo on p. 87, Barney is standing behind Gil,
manager Charlie Dressen is to his right, and Walter O'Malley
is to his left. Pee Wee Reese, George Shuba, and I are peering
over O'Malley's shoulder.

Party Time

T he Dodgers of the 1950s were not accustomed to losing.
Champions in 1952, 1953, 1955, and 1956 and near
misses in 1950, 1951, and 1954, the Dodgers were
always at or near the top. So whenever we would lose two games
in a row, things got serious.

Barney Stein (third from left) gets some help as he shows off his award-winning photo of first baseman Gil Hodges. *(Carl Erskine Collection)*

On one such occasion, Charlie Dressen, our manager, had a team meeting and chewed us out royally. We then lost our third in a row. Then Charlie used his sweet-talk treatment, telling us how great we were, real pros: "Now go out there and win this one." We lost our fourth straight. After the game, Dressen ordered our clubhouse man, John Griffin, to lock the door. No writers, no visitors. Then he instructed John to get out the "good stuff." Griff thought he meant for him to open the beer cooler, which was never available unless we won. Charlie yelled, "No, get the good stuff!" This meant the hard liquor, which John had stashed away and used only for writers or guests in the manager's office. So on the equipment trunks, John set out the scotch, bourbon, vodka, and Dressen's favorite, Harveys Bristol Cream sherry. Charlie called me to one side and said, "This is not for you. You're driving your buddies home to Bay Ridge." That was Preacher Roe, Pee Wee Reese, Duke Snider, and Rube Walker. Then he added: "And you're pitching tomorrow."

During the next hour, our team got real loose and real loud. Finally, at about 1:30 a.m., the party was over. When I let Preach out at his house, he was singing at the top of his voice. The next day he said he couldn't understand how Mozee heard him come in because he had taken his shoes off.

The next day we beat the Phillies 5-1 and went on to win the National League pennant. Although the New York writers got wind of the private party, they never wrote about it. They observed the old rule sometimes posted in the clubhouse, "What you see here, what you hear here, stays here."

Tex Rickards

Another Ebbets Field personality was Tex Rickards. Tex was the field announcer, and he would sit just outside the end of our dugout. He would announce the lineups and substitutions. He also made special announcements during the game when necessary. Many were classic: "Attention! Attention, please! There has been a kid found lost. Please claim him at the lost and found."

"Attention! Attention, please!" Pause—then, in a loud, commanding voice, "Hey, will you people in the left field stands please remove your coats from the rail and leave them there!"

A Cut Above

Brooklyn always took care of its Dodgers. Our butcher was Joe Rossi. One of our favorite nights out was to go to Joe's house for a four-hour Italian dinner. Betty learned a whole new set of great recipes and carried them back to our home in Indiana.

Years after my playing days, whenever I would go to New York City, I would call Joe Rossi in Brooklyn or his son Freddie and order 10 pounds of veal cutlet. Believe me, no one knows how to trim out a veal cutlet like an Italian butcher.

The Rossis would meet me at the airport and deliver the package. Back home in Indiana, we ate just as we did at Joe Rossi's house in Brooklyn.

Whitey

When a pitcher gets a starting assignment, one of three things will happen: a win, a loss, or a no-decision. If you happen to be facing Whitey Ford in a World Series, the odds change. It's more likely you'll get a loss. Whitey holds the record for most World Series wins—10.

Guess who holds the record for the most World Series losses? Whitey Ford, with eight. That means he also holds the record for most decisions (18), most starts (22), most innings

Comedian Phil Foster (left), "Brooklyn's Ambassador to the
World," and field announcer Tex Rickards at Ebbets Field.
(Courtesy of the Dodgers)

pitched (146), and most strikeouts (94). His three shutouts are the second most in World Series history.

You might say Whitey had a whole second career just in World Series play.

Failure Can Be Good

One of the greatest teams was the 1953 Dodgers. In all categories that team had great stats. Campy, Duke, and Hodges each drove in more than 125 runs. Jackie hit .329, Duke hit 40 home runs, and I personally had my best season, leading the National League with a 20-6 record. We won the pennant by several games.

Charlie Dressen, our manager, told me I would start the World Series and probably pitch three games if the Series went seven games.

The 1953 Series opened in Yankee Stadium. Well, as sometimes happens, I had a bad first inning. Not Mantle, not Berra, not Mize, but that little brat Billy Martin tripled off me with the bases loaded. I was taken out. What a disappointment! I had really failed my team and Dodgers fans.

After the game and our loss, Dressen called me aside and said, "I'm gonna start you in Game 3." Boy, was I surprised. With no travel day scheduled in between, that meant one day between starts.

I told Duke Snider, my roommate, that I was going to pitch that first inning like there was no tomorrow. The Yankees weren't going to get me out early. I had great determination not to fail again.

It was a tough game, 1-1, then 2-2 going into the eighth inning. Campy hit a homer off of Vic Raschi to give us a 3-2 lead and the ballgame.

After the game, there was celebration in the Dodger clubhouse. There was a crowd around my locker. Preacher Roe

This is my favorite photo—getting a kiss from my wife, Betty, after setting the World Series' strikeout record in 1953. *(Carl Erskine Collection)*

pushed his way in, shook my hand, and said, "Great game! Do you know you set a World Series strikeout record?" "No," I said. "Fourteen," said Preacher. "Mize in the ninth was your fourteenth." I was so busy, so determined to beat a great Yankee team, that I wasn't counting strikeouts.

That failure in Game 1 pushed me to do something I hadn't done at any level of pro baseball (i.e., strike out 14 batters in a game)—and it happened to be in the World Series.

It just goes to show it's not what happens to you, but what you do with what happens to you.

Incidentally, this happened on October 2, 1953. Sandy Koufax broke my record on October 2, 1963, with 15 Ks. Bob Gibson broke Sandy's record on October 2, 1968, with 17.

Edward R. Murrow

In the early days of television, Edward R. Murrow was launching a new live TV show called *Person to Person*, which was probably the first show to interview celebrities in their own homes. The first guest was Roy Campanella from his home on Long Island, an estate once owned by J.P. Morgan.

The date for the show was Saturday, October 2, 1953, which happened to coincide with the third game of the 1953 World Series.

At a rehearsal on the Friday evening following Game 2, Murrow told Roy that everything was ready, the show looked good. "Now," he said, "all you have to do, Roy, is hit a home run to win the game tomorrow and then come on my first show."

In the eighth inning, with the score tied 2-2, Campy hit a homer off of Vic Raschi to win the game, 3-2.

Edward R. Murrow's *Person to Person* became an award-winning TV series.

After Game 3 of the 1953 World Series, I celebrate striking out 14 Yankees to set a World Series strikeout record. *(Carl Erskine Collection)*

Knock, Knock

One of the pitches most often talked about is variously described as the knockdown, the beanball, the brushback, or the "stick it in his ear" pitch. On this type of delivery, the home plate umpire must make a judgment call as to whether it was intentional or accidental. Some of the best acting is not on stage but on the pitching mound after a pitcher throws a knockdown pitch.

It is an unwritten rule that a pitcher is expected to protect his own hitters and to retaliate if it appears that the opposing pitcher has intentionally thrown at a teammate. Managers Charlie Dressen and Leo Durocher had an interesting philosophy: "Give 'em two for one." When the Dodgers played the Giants, a low-run game might last three hours. I was ordered on several occasions to "knock the hitter down." This usually means a pitch thrown behind the hitter and above his shoulders. There's no place for him to go but down.

During the 1953 World Series, Charlie Dressen called me aside before the game and said, "Yogi is digging in; we got to loosen him up. Get a strike on him, and I want him on his back." It's always harder to complete a task correctly if it's somebody else's idea. My first try at decking Yogi was a pitch inside that hit him in the ribs. Of course, he was awarded first base. Dressen told me between innings that he wanted it done right, "so next time I want him down."

On Yogi's second time up, after a called strike, I got the knockdown sign from Campy. This time the pitch was up and inside. Yogi only turned away and the ball struck him hard on the elbow. He stared at me as he trotted to first base.

I happened to be the leadoff hitter the next inning. When I stepped into the batter's box, I expected Yogi to be pretty mad. All he did was look up at me through his mask and in a soft, deep voice, he said, "Carl, are you throwin' at me?"

I take part in the Chippewa Tribe induction ceremony in Namaha, Michigan. *(Carl Erskine Collection)*

Big Chief

After the 1953 World Series, I was inducted into the Chippewa Tribe in Namaha, Michigan, by Chief Antone Starr. I was given an Indian name, Bequaguad, which means "Mr. Baseball."

1954 Raise

In 1953, my sixth major league season, I had my only 20-win season (20-6) and won a World Series game. Naturally, I was expecting a good raise. I was making $18,000. Hank Greenberg, general manager for Cleveland, bet Buzzie Bavasi, general manager of the Dodgers, $10 that he wouldn't pay me what I asked for. Buzzie called me aside where we had been chatting in the lobby of an Atlanta hotel during the winter meeting. He said to me, "What do you want?" I said $30,000. Buzzie gave me the full shock treatment. "Oh, my, Carl, I couldn't do that." I said, "OK, pay Greenberg." Buzzie said, "Now wait a minute, let's talk. We've never had any trouble getting together." He said, "$28,500, and that's tops." I said, "Go pay Greenberg." "No, now wait," said Buzzie. "Here's what I'll do. You bring your family to spring training, so let me pick up their expenses—there's your $30,000."

"Not quite," I said. "That usually costs me less than $1,000." Now I'm trying to think of some way to get that last $500 to $600, so I say, "Buzzie, how about paying for the dental work I'm having done back in Anderson in the winter?"

He finally agreed. My dentist loved getting those Dodger checks, and he put six gold inlays in my teeth. Recently, I had to have one pulled. I saved the gold nugget and had a tie tack made out of it. If you see me dressed with a shirt and tie, I'll show you what's left of my 1954 raise.

Having a Calm-plex

Duing the season Betty and I often attended Marble Collegiate Church in Manhattan where Dr. Norman Vincent Peale was the senior pastor. Dr. Peale and I were good friends, so when the church, which was founded in the 1600s, was celebrating the 100th anniversary of its current building and sanctuary, I was asked me to speak at the banquet during the off season. It was a large affair. I made the trip to New York City, checked into a hotel, dressed in my tux, and proceeded to the ballroom. The head table was loaded with dignitaries, but for me the kicker was meeting the master of ceremonies, Lowell Thomas.

As a child, I had heard his famous voice every evening on the radio at 6:00 p.m. when he read the news. My father never missed his broadcast.

One by one Thomas introduced the various speakers. I was naturally a little tense. But when his famous voice started introducing me, my heart began to pound so hard that I thought it would burst through my shirt. I was fearful that I would not be able to speak. I had to do something fast.

And so in just a few seconds, I used one of Dr. Peale's famous positive thinking techniques—he said when pressure overwhelms you, just go back in your mind to the most peaceful experience that you can remember; dwell on it, and you become as calm as you were in your memory. My thoughts went back to earlier that day, in the morning, when I was at home in Anderson, Indiana. I had slipped into my sons' bedroom to kiss my five-year-old, Danny, and my three-year-old, Gary, good-bye. As I looked at my two little boys, so innocent and so peaceful, sleeping in their bunk beds, I saw complete tranquility. I was back in that scene in my mind.

Before Thomas had finished my introduction, I was completely calm. I walked to the mike, made my short remarks, and received a standing ovation.

That's the power of Dr. Peale's positive thinking.

Don Newcombe

In 1954 Don Newcombe returned to the Dodgers after spending the previous two seasons in the army. Missing those two years during the peak of his career probably cost him a place in the Hall of Fame. After all, he'd been Rookie of the Year, Most Valuable Player, and one of the first Cy Young Award winners.

Jackie Robinson had been in the league since 1947 but was still not welcome at the Park Chase Hotel in St. Louis. The black players stayed in another hotel for blacks only. Newcombe said to Jackie, "I just did a tour of military duty for this country and can't even stay in the same hotel with my team. Let's go talk to the manager of the Park Chase Hotel."

The manager of the hotel was cordial but said, "Well, you fellas can't stay here because we don't want you out around the swimming pool." Newk said, "Who wants to swim? We just want to stay with our team." It was granted, with this proviso: "You can't eat in the dining room. You'll take room service." That last barrier didn't come down until the next year.

Dizzy

One of the early players-turned-broadcaster was Dizzy Dean. His down-home language and homespun humor made him very popular. English teachers, however, cringed at his poor grammar and used to write him letters strongly criticizing his use or misuse of words. His reply was, "A lot of teachers who ain't sayin' ain't, ain't eatin'."

Dizzy's description of Cincinnati first baseman Ted Kluszewski was a classic. Ted's arms were so big that he had to cut the sleeves of his uniform off at the shoulders. His mammoth bare arms were exposed all the way up.

As Ted approached the plate one day, Dean said, "Hold it, folks, here comes a feller up to hit with his legs coming out of his shirtsleeves."

The Towel

There are lots of subtle advantages to playing in your home park. In St. Louis the infield was very hard, except on nights when sinkerballer Jerry Staley pitched. On those occasions, the grounds crew would wet down the area in front of home plate so that opposing batters would beat that sinker into soft turf for easy ground balls.

In Ebbets Field our bullpen was down the right field line. The bullpen bench was against the wall, just in foul territory. The right field fence was only 297 feet from home plate but had a 30-foot-high screen.

The player in the bullpen who sat next to the foul line had an important daily assignment that required him to keep a towel on his lap and stay ready. With men on base for the Dodgers and less than two outs and a fly ball hit to right field, the runners couldn't tell whether the right fielder could catch the fly ball or whether it would hit the fence above him for a base hit. Our man with the towel could see that easily. Whenever the ball was going to hit the fence above the fielder, our man would wave the towel, and all of the runners would go. We scored many a winning run with this home field advantage.

Mickey Vernon

The All-Star Game in 1954 was played in Cleveland. With the score tied, 9-9, I was called in to pitch in the eighth inning. The bases were loaded with nobody out. The hitter was Mickey Vernon, a premier hitter and a real tough guy to strike out. We had never faced each other. Smokey Burgess was catching, and when I ran the count to three balls and one strike, Smokey called for my straight change, a pitch not many hitters would see in that situation. I threw him a beauty for strike two. It was such a surprise to Mickey that he took the next fastball for strike three.

I hadn't seen Mickey for over 25 years until I was at Yankee Stadium for an Old-Timers' Game weekend. I was visiting with several other old-timers in the hospitality suite when Mickey Vernon walked in. A tall, straight, very dignified gentleman, but one not given to much talk, Mickey looked around the room, then walked slowly over to me, leaned down, and said quietly in my ear, "That was one helluva pitch."

Noticed

During the 1950s New York was the center of the boxing world or at least had a strong identity with the sport. Harlem was home to one of the most popular fighters in his day—Sugar Ray Robinson. Sugar Ray was a champion middleweight and one of the most handsome and best-dressed athletes in the sports world. As if he needed more attention, he owned a big Easter-egg lavender Cadillac. When that Caddy drove down 125th Street in Harlem, everybody knew Sugar Ray was in town.

Roy Campanella was at the top of his game in baseball and decided to open a liquor store in Harlem on 125th Street.

His store had a signature six-year-old bourbon whiskey called Campy's Old Peg. (I was always surprised that baseball permitted Campy to own a liquor store because there were restrictions on active players endorsing hard liquor.)

But not to be outdone by Sugar Ray, Campy bought an El Dorado Cadillac and had it painted gold—Incan gold. Whenever the folks in Harlem saw that gold Caddy, they knew Campy was there and hurried in for an autograph and maybe a bottle.

Ben Wade

Ben Wade, a good right-handed pitcher for the Dodgers in the mid-1950s, was hard of hearing but was a great kidder. He called everyone "Virgil."

We were returning from a two-week road trip, and everyone was anxious to get home. As we circled LaGuardia Airport, we all knew that our sweet, young, and beautiful wives would be waiting to welcome us home. Ben was married to a very petite and beautiful girl named Betsy.

Ben turned to me as we deplaned and said, "Hey, Virgil, when I get home, the second thing I'm gonna do is set my bag down."

It's How You See It

To say umpires are just human would get a big rise out of some players and managers. An umpire's judgment not only can affect the outcome of the game, but over time affects a player's statistics, either favorably or unfavorably. The old baseball saying is, "They even up." But no one can prove or disprove that. The only truth to the matter is that players take an umpire's decision very personally.

On the other hand, the umpires are trying to remain unemotional and make the calls. As Hall of Fame umpire Al Barlich said, "On a close pitch the hitter wants it, the pitcher wants it—I don't care who gets it." The most difficult situation for an umpire or a team is when two umpires make opposite calls on the same play.

This happened in Philadelphia with big Don Newcombe pitching to Stan Lopata. Lopata hit a long drive down the left field line close to the foul pole. As the ball hooked past the pole, umpire Lou Warneke, working the left field foul line signaled fair ball. Home plate umpire Vic Delmar, who was watching the ball and not Warneke, called it foul.

Newcombe, who had been watching the ball and only seen Warneke's call, was stunned. To him, it was obviously foul, not a home run. As he starred at Warneke, Delmar reached into his uniform pocket to put a new ball into play and threw it at the mound. Newk never saw the ball coming; it struck him squarely on the head, and he dropped to his knees.

I was in the bullpen with the other pitchers, and we were listening to Gene Kelly, the Phillies' broadcaster, describe what was taking place right before our eyes. Kelly hadn't seen Delmar hit Newk with the ball, so when he saw Newk down on the mound, he said, "That home run really shook up Newcombe. He's down on his knees with his head in his hands and appears to be ill."

After Kelly's comment, the entire bullpen was filled with hysterical laughter. It was a good thing that our manager couldn't see us because we would have been hard pressed to explain our hysterics over a Phillies home run.

On the field, Delmar did not overrule Warneke because Warneke was closer to the play. Newk composed himself and finished the game, but the radio audience never got the full story.

In the clubhouse after the game, Newk wasn't icing his pitching arm (as is common practice in baseball today). Instead he was icing the knot on his head.

All Things Work Together

There is a linkage in life that sometimes requires a long look back to see how it connects.

I was a kid playing baseball in a vacant lot. A man named John Perry stopped by one day and asked all of us to come to his Sunday School at First Baptist Church. We resisted and said we liked just being with our buddies. He said, "OK, we'll start a class just for you boys." I got active in the church and during Youth Sunday was elected deacon for the day. Later, when I went into pro baseball, that church connection followed me. In 1952, *Guideposts* magazine was new, and its managing editor, Len Lasourde, interviewed me for an article called "The Inside Pitch." It basically dealt with my personal faith and belief in God.

Down in Oklahoma, a high school basketball coach and church layman, Don McClanen, was collecting any articles he could find on pro athletes who expressed a wholesome religious lifestyle. In 1954 Don approached me in the lobby of the Warwick Hotel in Philadelphia. I had just come off my best big-league season, and the "red-hot" deals were coming my way. I had learned to be wary of most of them. McClanen, however, was so soft-spoken and laid back that he impressed me. When he told me of his idea to organize pro athletes to speak at high schools, colleges, and other youth settings—endorsing their faith and church relationship—I listened with a different kind of interest. He had already contacted football greats Otto Graham and Doak Walker because of articles he had collected.

This encounter and the subsequent enlisting of other athletes from all sports marked the birth of the Fellowship of Christian Athletes.

The FCA has become a significant force in helping youngsters, coaches, their families, and others develop a wholesome and disciplined lifestyle as an arm of the church. In the years that followed the FCA's inception, a more spiritual openness began to develop in baseball. Currently, most major and minor league teams have baseball chapel on a regular weekly basis—right in the clubhouse. Players and their families attend spiritual retreats. Coaches lead huddle groups in schools and colleges.

Major league baseball was blessed with several outstanding players who helped the FCA in its formative years. Among them were Robin Roberts, Alvin Dark, George Kell, Vernon Law, Brooks Robinson, and Bobby Richardson. Branch Rickey assumed the role of founder and financial supporter.

One of the biggest dividends I earned from my baseball years is to be in a city anywhere in the country and see a boy or a girl riding a bike and wearing an FCA T-shirt—more than 40 years after I first met Don McClanen.

Preach and Quitting

One of the craftiest and best control pitchers of the 1940s and 1950s was Preacher Roe, a tall, slim, left-handed country boy from Hardy, Arkansas. Campy used to say, "Who's pitching today?" "Preacher," someone answered. "Well," said Roy, "they can cut the middle of the plate out and throw it away—ol' Preach ain't gonna use it."

Preacher played down his fastball, calling it his burner, but he had a good fastball. Not only was he a crafty pitcher, but he was just as clever at making sage observations or telling a yarn. He retired at the end of the 1954 season.

Preacher told us he knew exactly when it was time for him to quit. It was a hot night in St. Louis, late in the game, and he was facing Stan Musial. Preach said, "I was old, I was tired, and I was facing the best hitter in the National League. I reached back to get the last bit of good stuff I had. My burner got away from me and was heading right at Stan's head." Preach went on, "Fellows, I had time to yell, 'Look out!' three times before it got there."

A bit of advice from Preacher: "Live every day like it's your last. Someday you'll be right."

Barnstorming Whitey and Harvey

It was always great to go on a postseason barnstorming tour because it was usually like an All-Star team with players from different teams and different leagues involved. Such a team was headed for Hawaii in 1954 to play a series of games. Most of our wives accompanied us. A few players were without their wives and had an unending bachelor party.

As we boarded the plane in San Francisco, Whitey Ford and Harvey Kuenn had a nice buzz on and planned to continue with the cooler of beer they brought aboard. Seated near us was a couple obviously starting on their honeymoon. They were cuddling in the seat across the aisle from Harvey and Whitey. They, too, were a little tipsy from the champagne reception they had just left.

When Whitey saw the big corsage and recognized that they were honeymooners, he said, "Hey, Harv, let's kiss the bride." Both Harvey and Whitey took turns embracing the little bride in the aisle; they gave her several kisses. She seemed to enjoy it and didn't resist. That prompted more of the same. By this time, the groom was plenty irritated. Before we ever left the ground, the honeymooners had their first real spat and weren't speaking. By the time we landed in Honolulu, the good-natured Whitey and Harvey had them laughing and hugging again.

Straight Talk

One of my chief rivals was Robin Roberts, pitcher for the Philadelphia Phillies. During the 1950s, as Roberts was accumulating Hall of Fame stats, we faced each other many times. Although the Dodgers beat him occasionally, he was a consistent 20-game winner and pitched more than 300 innings year after year.

Despite our rivalry, Robin once said something that gave me a new perspective on my life.

Robin and I were the very first athletes to represent the Fellowship of Christian Athletes. It was at a high school convocation in Oklahoma City in 1954. We were there in the off season at the request of Don McClanen, founder of the FCA.

We had no script or notes, no format to follow. We were on our own to speak about our faith to these high school students. It was a tense time and made us both more nervous than we were before starting a game.

Robin was first. What he said was very simple, yet very profound. "When I was a teenager," he said, "I found that I could throw a baseball real hard—harder than my buddies. I figured I'd been given this unique talent, so I said that since God has given me this ability, He should have something to say about how I use it."

Trivia Records

The Brooklyn Dodgers of the 1950s had a strong and powerful right-handed-hitting lineup. One of the toughest pitchers in the league for right-handers was Ewell "The Whip" Blackwell. He usually pitched low-hit, low-run games against us.

However, one day at Ebbets Field, a most unusual inning occurred. Blackwell gave up a bunch of runs in the first inning and was relieved. Once the powerful Dodger lineup got into the Reds' bullpen, the runs piled up: 15 runs in the first inning with 12 of those scored after two were out. Chris Van Cuyk, our starting pitcher, has to own a trivia record. Van Cuyk, batting in the ninth position, got two singles in the first inning.

In another interesting bit of trivia, relief specialist Clem Labine, a lifetime .075 hitter, got just three hits for the entire 1955 season—all three were home runs.

Green Grass of Home

Around 1950, television began to revolutionize the game of baseball. TV now produces more revenue than all other sources and, along with free agency, has given players the opportunity for multimillion-dollar contracts.

In 1955 the Dodger payroll was the largest in the league, but still, it totaled less than $1 million. Jackie Robinson, Duke Snider, Pee Wee Reese, and Roy Campanella—each a Hall of Famer—never made as much as $50,000 in any one year. In stark contrast, the Dodgers' payroll in 1999 exceeded $80 million. One of the reasons is that, prior to the 1998 season, the Dodgers signed free agent pitcher Kevin Brown to a seven-year contract worth $105 million.

Color television was introduced in the mid-1950s and was sensational. Ballparks back then had very colorful billboards around their outfield fences. The color was amazing.

One major problem was immediately evident. The grass was green, but bare spots showed up in ugly patches—mostly in front of home plate, where batted balls hit the ground, and also in those areas where players consistently warmed up. The solution was to spray paint the bare spots green. On camera, the field looked fine.

C. Oscar Johnson

I was accustomed to attending church on Sunday morning, but that was difficult during the baseball season. Whenever possible, I would find a church near the hotel, get permission to arrive at the ballpark late (if I wasn't scheduled to pitch that day), and then attend an early church service.

In St. Louis I would go to the Third Baptist Church on Grand Avenue, where C. Oscar Johnson, a strong Baptist minister, was pastor.

During the service, he would spot me and, in his big, booming voice, ask me to stand, introduce me, and cause me to feel quite embarrassed. This happened two or three more times on subsequent trips to St. Louis. The experience actually made me reluctant to go back.

However, one Sunday, during a later trip to St. Louis, I asked Walt Alston permission to be late so I could attend church. I decided to go back to the same church because it was on Grand Avenue, the same street as the ballpark. I entered through the side door, quickly sit down, and hoped I wasn't noticed.

During the service, C. Oscar Johnson said, "Well, folks, we have an outstanding major league player here today—good family man and strong church man. He often comes here when he can work it into his baseball schedule." My face and neck began to get hot. I knew what was coming next. He then said, "I'm going to have him stand right now—Alvin Dark, up there in the balcony." Actually, at that moment, I felt worse than I did whenever he introduced me.

Granny Hamner

Baseball players never miss a chance to needle the opposition, sometimes sticking that needle in really deep.

In a close game at Ebbets Field against the "Whiz Kid" Phillies, I fell victim to what I thought were three bad calls in a row, which, in turn, cost me the game. With the score tied, 2-2, in the ninth, I ran the count to 3-2 on Granny Hamner, the scrappy little shortstop for the Phillies. The next pitch appeared to be strike three, but Artie Gore, umpiring behind home plate, called it ball four. Hamner walked. A couple of pitches later, Hamner attempted to steal second. Campy's throw was on the money—we had him. No, we didn't. Dusty Boggess, umpiring at second, called Hamner safe. Now I had to face Willie "Puddin' Head" Jones, the Phillies' third baseman. Willie hit a line drive to center for a base hit. Duke Snider, in center, fired the ball home to cut down Hamner trying to score. It was a great throw, a close play, and Campy clearly tagged Hamner out. Not so! The call was "safe." We lost, 3-2.

The next day, Artie Gore saw me near the clubhouse before game time. He said, "Carl, I missed that strike on Hamner." Well, that was little consolation but part of the game. It wasn't until I saw Hamner during infield practice that I really got the "jab." He walked past me on the field and said, "Carl, just for the record, I was out all three places."

Sticky, Sticky Goo

For decades, the only foreign substance used in baseball was rosin. Both batters and pitchers were permitted to use it to assist them in gripping the bat or the baseball.

Ralph Kiner was a premier home run hitter, and we all noticed that he used a piece of towel to wipe his bat handle while in the on-deck circle. We sent our batboy over to the Pirates' bench one day to swipe this rag and see what he was using. It was pine tar—a thick, sticky, black substance worked into the towel, along with the rosin, to really improve the grip.

Gil Hodges picked up on this idea quickly and had Charlie "The Brow" fix a pine tar rag. Gil used a lot of the stuff, and his hands at the end of a game were black. Soap and water would not remove it, so he kept a jar of mechanic's compound in his locker to strip his hands clean. Pine tar is legal if kept only on the handle of the bat, not on the barrel.

During a game, Hodges would come to the mound, bringing the ball after a putout at first base. He would give the ball a couple of good, hard squeezes with those big hands of his. When he handed me the ball, it was nice and sticky. For the next few pitches, I would benefit from an extra-good grip, especially with my curveball. A new ball would come into play after a foul ball.

Pitchers also got to bat, which gave them a legal opportunity to apply a good bit of pine tar to their hands, which usually lasted through the next inning.

Swifty

There were two players in the National League who were known for their lack of speed: Rube Walker, the catcher for the Dodgers, and Del Rice, the catcher for the St. Louis Cardinals. On a trip to St. Louis, the Dodgers passed the Cardinals, who were on the field for batting practice, and the debate about whose catcher was slower began. We decided that we would settle it once and for all in a 50-yard race.

Both teams moved to the outfield, and the two rather unwilling participants began to "rev up" for the race. As Walker took off his spikes so that he could run better on the outfield grass and Rice flexed his legs and practiced some starts, some placed their bets. The 50 yards were laid out from center field to the right foul line. Finally, all was ready.

"Get on your mark, get set, go!"

The lead-footed catchers sprinted across the outfield, and Rice won the race by three yards. Walker apologized to his teammates, and the Dodgers were forced to pay up.

Later, Warren Giles, the National League president, heard about the race and reprimanded both clubs for their inappropriate behavior. But the matter was settled in both teams' minds.

Fresco Thompson, the vice president for the Dodgers, once commented on Walker's running speed, "Rube will fool you. He's slower than he looks."

He definitely proved it at Sportsman's Park that day.

"The Brow"

Another Ebbets Field character was Charlie "The Brow" DiGiovanna. Charlie was an Italian street kid from Brooklyn and our batboy. Later he became an assistant in the clubhouse. He had a heavy Brooklyn accent and was devoted to all of those Dodger greats. He delighted in cleaning and shining our shoes.

Charlie was also responsible for getting some six dozen baseballs signed daily. If some players missed signing the balls, which the club used for various promotions, Charlie would catch a blast from his boss, "Big" John Griffin.

Charlie was smart. He learned how to substitute a signature if his neck was on the line. Out there somewhere are a few bogus signatures penned by the skillful hand of Charlie "The Brow."

Charlie "The Brow" DiGiovanna gets a soda pop shower from me after the Dodgers won the 1955 World Series. *(Carl Erskine Collection)*

The Presidents

A great American tradition is having the president of the United States throw out the first pitch to start a new season. During my playing years, presidents Truman, Eisenhower, and Nixon (who was vice president then), as well as one of the former presidents, Herbert Hoover, all came to Ebbets Field.

The players and coaches were well aware of a president's visit because federal agents were stationed in every part of Ebbets Field.

To me, the all-time greatest quote by any baseball player was uttered by Babe Ruth in 1930. Ruth was being signed by Yankees owner Colonel Jacob Ruppert for a record $80,000, following a season in which Ruth had batted .359, slugged 49 homers, and driven in 153 runs. In a press conference, the Babe was asked how it felt to be making more money than the president of the United States. Ruth replied, "I had a better year than Hoover." Hoover, of course, was our president during the early days of the Great Depression, which had begun in 1929.

The Buckle

In the off season I was encouraged by some hometown friends to petition the Masonic Lodge, Fellowship Lodge 681, in Anderson, Indiana. I did petition the lodge and went through the steps to become a Mason. The Masonic Order is based on Old Testament scripture and has God at the center of all its activities. The well recognized symbol of The Order is a square and compass with a large "G" in the center.

When I returned to the Dodgers the next spring, I lockered next to our rookie second baseman, Jim Gilliam. One day Jim wore a beautiful Masonic buckle. Of course, I noticed it right

I chat with former president Herbert Hoover at the 1949 World Series. *(Carl Erskine Collection)*

I talk to Richard Nixon, who was running for vice president at the time, after an 11th-inning victory in Game 5 of the 1952 World Series at Yankee Stadium. *(Carl Erskine Collection)*

away. I wanted to engage him in conversation, but being a new Mason myself, I was reluctant. A day or two later, Jim wore the buckle again. This time I said, "Hey, Jim, good-looking belt buckle." He said, "Yes, I really like it." I said, "I guess it has a lot of meaning for you." "Oh, yes," he said. "I saw this in a store window in Chicago and went right in and bought it. I think it's great. It has my initial right in the middle."

Happy Days

Happy Felton had three shows daily at Ebbets Field before home games. One of the most remembered experiences for Little Leaguers was to appear on *Happy Felton's Knot Hole Gang* and get to meet their favorite Dodgers. There was a pregame show in the Dodgers' bullpen where three Little Leaguers fielded ground balls, caught fly balls, and threw to a Dodger player. The player then would pick who he thought was the best and that youngster got to go to the second show, a dugout show where the kid could talk to any Dodger player he chose. Felton's postgame show was called *Talk to the Stars*, a phone-in show for fans to talk to the star of the game from each team.

Happy Felton was also a big-game fisherman and had patches, trophies, and pictures of his many catches of marlin, sailfish, and big tuna. During spring training Felton would charter a fishing boat out of Miami and take a few Dodgers out for the day in the Gulf Stream. He told us we could have any strike unless it was a "billfish"—that was his.

On one trip we trolled into a school of kingfish, which are strong swimmers and good fighters. Gil Hodges was having a field day catching twenty-pounders. Each catch took several minutes and lots of strength to land, which eventually became a problem for Gil.

On one of many fishing trips, the successful fishermen—Gil Hodges, Larry McDonald, Carl Furillo, a crew member, me, the captain, and Happy Felton—display our catches from the sea. *(Carl Erskine Collection)*

See, we had a preseason game that night at Miami Stadium, and Gil was so sore from fishing that he could not take batting practice. During infield practice and the game itself he insisted that the infielders throw the ball below his belt—he couldn't lift his arms.

Jack in the Box

It's often said that the most exciting play in baseball is a triple. Fielders are chasing the ball, a relay is necessary, and the runner is going all out with usually a hard slide and close play at third. That play doesn't compare to my pick as the most exciting play to watch. For me, it was Jackie Robinson caught in a rundown between the bases.

Jackie was so quick, so elusive that even seasoned major league players looked like inept amateurs trying to catch him. Then, most often, Jackie would find a way to weave and dodge all tags and arrive safely on the base. The photo on the following page shows Jackie trapped on the third base line at Ebbets Field with seemingly no way out. The Philadelphia Phillies also thought they had him. Actually, Jackie scored on this play.

King Karl

In 1954 the Dodgers finished the season behind the first-place New York Giants. Although the pennant had been decided, we still had a series with the Giants and the Pirates. This was a time when a manager could give young, talented hopefuls a shot. Karl Spooner was a left-handed pitcher with an amazing fastball and deceptive delivery. He got his chance to start against the Giants.

He was very wild, walking the bases loaded and falling behind hitter Willie Mays three balls and one strike. Manager

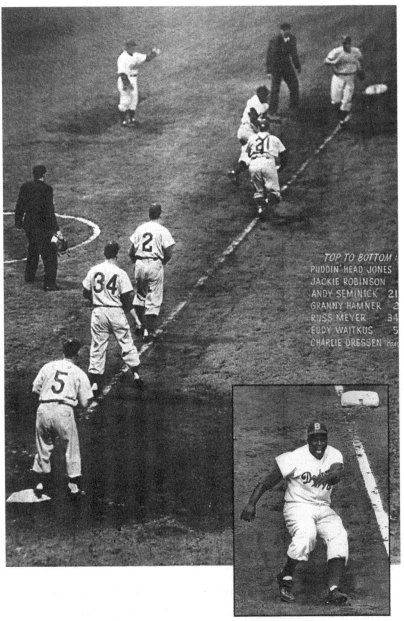

TOP TO BOTTOM :
PUDDIN' HEAD JONES
JACKIE ROBINSON
ANDY SEMINICK 21
GRANNY HAMNER 2
RUSS MEYER 34
EDDY WAITKUS 5
CHARLIE DRESSEN coach

Jackie Robinson actually escaped this rundown and scored.
(Courtesy of the Dodgers; inset photo courtesy of Sal Larocca)

Walt Alston said at that point, "If he walks him, go get him, Joe." Joe Becker was the pitching coach, but he didn't step on the field that inning. Spooner threw a strike. With the count 3-2, Mays swung and missed a high fastball well above the strike zone. Spooner got out of the inning. He went on to shut out the Giants and strike out 15, retiring six consecutive batters with Ks at one point in the game. In the last series against Pittsburgh, he shut out the Pirates and struck out 12. He totaled two wins, two shutouts, two complete games, and 27 strikeouts. The season was over, and because the Dodgers had not won the pennant, much emphasis was put on this new pitching phenom, Karl Spooner. The press dubbed him "King Karl, the strikeout king."

Even later Roy Campanella, who caught for many talented pitchers, witnessed the power Spooner packed. In his book, *It's Good to be Alive*, he wrote, "The best-pitched game I ever caught was Carl Erskine's World Series victory over the Yankees when he struck our 14 batters. He was really fast that day, but the pitcher who was absolutely the fastest I ever caught was Karl Spooner. Nobody ever threw harder than that kid did in those first two games he pitched in the majors."

In spring training in 1955, Spooner was big news. When we finished our 10 days of training at Vero Beach, Florida, we moved to Miami to open our spring training season. During a Sunday afternoon game against the Detroit Tigers, Johnny Podres was the starting pitcher. He was expected to pitch just three innings, but after two innings Podres told Alston that his shoulder was tender and he felt he shouldn't push it by going another inning. So while the Dodgers went to bat, Alston said, "Get Spooner up in the bullpen." But the Dodgers at bat were taken out one, two, three. Spooner was summoned to the mound.

"Now coming to pitch is the sensational young pitcher, Strikeout King Karl Spooner," the announcer boomed.

Naturally Spooner was pumped up, but he wasn't really warmed up. He cut loose on his best fastball and then another. That's when something snapped. He had injured his shoulder.

In those few moments one of the great arms of Dodger pitching had lost its magic. Spooner was used on and off again after that, but he never regained that unhittable stuff he was born with.

For every great pitcher who makes the majors there is an uncounted number of great young arms lost in obscurity to early injuries. Most of these happened in the years before sports medicine and a better understanding of arm injuries. Also before the 1950s, coaches and managers were exclusively nonpitchers. There was no one on staff who really understood how a pitcher's arm felt. Unless there was blood or a bone showing, it was assumed that it was all in a pitcher's head. When I complained about a muscle pull in my shoulder, manager Burt Shotton, a former outfielder, told me the way to get a "kink" out of my arm was to go out to the center field flagpole and throw straight up at the flag.

Mike Fright

During a spring training game in West Palm Beach against the Philadelphia Athletics, I pitched the first three innings, did my required running, and was finished for the day. But club rules required that a player stay through the game.

To watch the rest of the game, I went up to the press box. Vin Scully was doing the broadcast and motioned for me to join him in the booth. As he did play by play, he would draw me in to comment on a pitch, a play, or some game strategy. I was a bit nervous but began to feel more comfortable and after a few innings even bolder. Just then Jim Gilliam hit an extra-base hit, a sure double that he stretched into a hard-sliding triple. I mentioned how important that extra base was and then said, "Well, Vin, you know there are ten ways you can score from third that you can't from second." Vince said, "Really, that's interesting.

What are the ten ways?" I started the list confidently: sacrifice
fly, infield hit, passed ball, wild pitch—then I slowed down—an
error . . . interference . . . a balk. Now I am dead, I can't think,
my mind is frozen with stage fright. I only named seven—what
are the other three?! Vince took me off the hook momentarily
with comments about the next pitch, but I never did name the
last three. Can you? See page 233 for the answers.

Music's Fine

D on Newcombe was big, hard-throwing, and the only
player of his time to be Rookie of the Year (1949),
Most Valuable Player (1956), and the Cy Young
Award winner (also 1956).

Big Newk loved music and carried a record player with
him on road trips. During a trip to Chicago, Newk pitched an
afternoon game and was ready for a little relaxation that night.
Our manager, Walt Alston, had the same concerns as all visiting
managers in Chicago—players free at night in that fun town.
Consequently, there was always a bed check about 1:00 a.m.

When Newk's room was checked, he was not there. At
2:00 a.m., still no Newk. Same results at 3:00 a.m.

The next day in the Wrigley Field clubhouse, Alston held
our usual pregame meeting. When that was finished, he turned
to Newk and confronted him with the question about where he
was the night before.

Newk finally admitted he was down the hall in another
room with friends listening to his records. Alston said, "Newk,
for what I'm going to fine you, you could have hired a three-
piece band. That's three hundred dollars!"

Gillette Me Tell You

One of the rowdiest and most famous fans at Ebbets Field was Hilda Chester. She had a gravel voice and a cowbell, and neither was ever quiet.

Hilda could really give it to a player having a bad day. Duke Snider and I left Ebbets Field after a night game loss. It was a game in which Duke had struck out twice and hit into a double play.

Hilda was waiting right at the clubhouse door, ready to pounce on Duke. She said, "Duke, you were lousy. You stink." We walked on, heading for our car, which was parked across Bedford Avenue. Hilda and her cowbell kept following us and razzing Duke. Under the light from the street lamp, we could make out Hilda's rough features and the fuzz on her chin. As we reached our car, Duke had held it in long enough. After another blast from Hilda, Duke said, "Ah, Hilda, why don't you go home and shave?"

It Happened in the Dark

Possibly the most popular player in Dodger history is Harold "Pee Wee" Reese. Even his nickname is magic, especially to youngsters.

There was great preparation and anticipation for his 30th birthday party at Ebbets Field. It happened at a night game on July 22, 1955. The pregame activities were like any other game. Only at the end of the fifth inning did the real purpose of the evening get underway.

The game was halted. Pee Wee, his wife Dottie, and daughter Barbie were escorted to home plate, and the tributes began to flow. The masters of ceremony were Vin Scully and Happy Felton. Messages were read from President Dwight D.

Eisenhower, Commissioner Ford Frick, New York Governor Harriman, and even Douglas MacArthur. As the player representative, I presented Pee Wee a silver tray with the autographs of all of his Dodgers teammates engraved on it.

Then through the center field gate came a stream of new automobiles. As they moved around the warning track and passed home plate, a fish bowl containing keys for each car was held out. Barbie reached in and drew a set of keys to the Chevrolet.

For the finale, a huge birthday cake was rolled out, the lights were turned down, and around 34,000 fans lit matches. The fans, lead by organist Gladys Gooding, sang "Happy Birthday" to their favorite Dodger. It was a tremendous outpouring of affection.

The lights were turned on. The teams took the field in the top of the sixth. What no one knew or suspected was now revealed. During the ceremony, the grounds crew, those unheralded men who kept Ebbets Field in great shape, had paid their own tribute to the "Little Colonel" from Louisville. They had gone to the roof where the eight pennants representing the eight teams in the National League waved and removed them. They had replaced them with Confederate flags to honor their friend.

The game ended with a Dodger win—an almost perfect night. But back in the clubhouse, Jackie Robinson was livid. He was so upset by the display of Confederate flags that he was loudly protesting in front of his locker. He denounced the act and continued to berate those responsible. Any attempt to console Jackie at this point was impossible; a few of us spoke with him and assured him we were on his side but thought that in this particular case he would lose more supporters than he would gain.

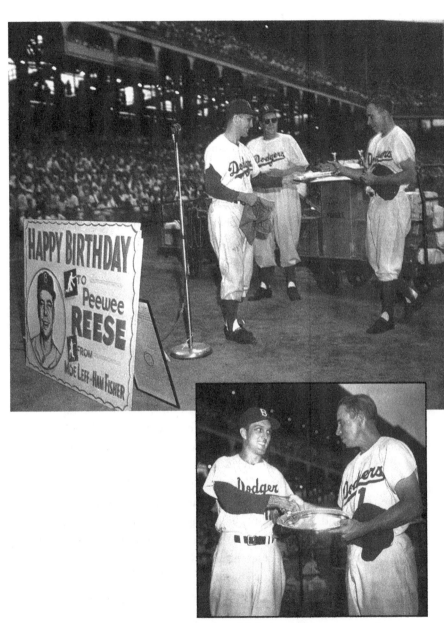

Pee Wee Reese receives his 30th birthday present from his teammates, a silver tray with each teammate's signature engraved on it. *(Carl Erskine Collection)*

Take That!

Gil Hodges was the biggest and strongest man of the Brooklyn Dodgers. Now that's a powerful statement considering that Carl Furillo, Jackie Robinson, and Roy Campanella were all big men. Gil was also the quietest man on the team—soft-spoken and more often not spoken. As rowdy as our bench was, I never heard Hodges yell an obscenity or even a mild barb at an opponent.

One thing about Gil did irritate his managers. He would never argue with an umpire. Being a first baseman, he had literally thousands of chances to challenge a close call. He never did. At the plate, Gil never questioned a called strike. One year he struck out 100 times. Seventy of those third strikes could have been argued as balls, but Gil never said a word. Manager Charlie Dressen told Gil if he would argue enough with an umpire to get ejected just once, he would give him $100. It never happened.

At Chicago's Wrigley Field, home plate umpire Tom Gorman called Gil out on a very low third strike. We could all see it from the dugout. Gil just walked calmly back to the dugout, gently placed his batting helmet on the bench, and coolly placed his bat in the bat rack. A few comments that Gil got robbed were directed his way.

On his next at-bat, Gorman again called Gil out on a questionable pitch. Gil responded the same way again. Now our bench and Walt Alston, the manager, were giving Gorman an earful. When Gil sat down, the barrage was directed at him.

"You've got to do something, Gil."

"He's taking the bat right out of your hands."

"He's taking bread and butter away from your family."

"You've got to defend yourself."

"You're too easy."

After several verbal blasts, Gil said, "Okay! Okay! Okay! The next time I'm up, I won't even ask Tom how his kids and wife are."

Cakewalk

Baseball is shot through with superstitions. Players, managers, and fans all get caught up at one time or another believing that where they sit, what they wear, or what is said affects the outcome of the game.

During the 1955 season, the Dodgers were again the favorites to win the National League pennant. About midseason, Frank Kellert received a package from his family in Oklahoma. It was a buttermilk cake. He shared it with the team before a game, and we won. The cake lasted long enough for us to win a couple more games. Sometime after that, the team went into a minor slump. Kellert was asked to contact his family for another buttermilk cake. The cakes kept coming, and we kept winning and clinched the pennant.

During the World Series, we had a supply of buttermilk cakes, and we beat the Yankees for the first and only world championship in the 75-year history of the Brooklyn Dodgers.

Here's the recipe for that buttermilk cake:

1 cup shortening
4 whole eggs
1 dash salt
1/2 tsp. baking soda (dissolved in buttermilk)
1 cup buttermilk
4 tbsp. vanilla
3 cups all-purpose flour
1 cup finely chopped pecans
2 cups sugar

Cream shortening and sugar together. Add eggs. Add flour and buttermilk alternately. Add vanilla, stir well, and add pecans. Bake in a well greased and floured tube pan at 350 degrees for one hour.

The Victory

The 1955 spring training season started in the same manner as many before. The Brooklyn Dodgers were coming off a string of good years and National League championships but still did not possess a World Series ring and trophy. The team had won the National League championships in 1890, 1899, 1900, 1916, 1920, 1941, 1947, 1949, 1952, and 1953, but never a World Series. Dodger fans were frustrated; Dodger players were bewildered. "We have a great team. Why can't we win?" It seemed that there was a barrier we just could not get through. But this team was not discouraged. When the regular season started, we were out of the gate fast and we never looked back. We clinched the pennant again and were going to face the New York Yankees and the ghost of Babe Ruth.

The series was a typical battle; after six games we were tied at three games each.

Young Johnny Podres started Game 7 and was masterful at shutting out the Yankees 2-0 for the first and only Brooklyn Dodgers World Series championship. When Elston Howard grounded out to Pee Wee Reese for the final out, our bench charged on to the field and mobbed Podres. To break through the barrier on the Yankees' home turf was even sweeter.

As we left the field and went up the runway to the clubhouse, it began to sink in just how significant the win was. It was truly a rare moment, so much so that as the team entered the locker room, there was a collective feeling of reverence—a quiet, reflective moment of true humility and gratitude, a spiritual moment that is hard to describe but deeply felt—before

Jim Gilliam, Carl Furillo, and Duke Snider join me for a scrumptious buttermilk cake. *(Carl Erskine Collection)*

the cork popped and the celebration began. That brief moment spoke volumes to me about the depth of character of this great Brooklyn team.

As for the loyal, long-suffering fans, no one slept in Flatbush that night. And to this day on October 4 at precisely 3:43 p.m., the very moment Pee Wee threw Elston Howard out on October 4, 1955, Brooklyn fans still gather annually near where Ebbets Field stood to count down to that moment and celebrate the 1955 World Series championship again and again.

Turnpike

The 1955 World Series was the ultimate highlight for Brooklyn Dodgers fans everywhere. To this day, Brooklyn baseball fans have an annual countdown at the exact hour and minute when Elston Howard grounded out to Pee Wee Reese for the final out of the seventh-game 2-0 victory.

Duke Snider and I left Brooklyn and drove west to Indiana, where Duke was going to spend a couple days with me on the golf course. As we zoomed down the Pennsylvania Turnpike, a state trooper pulled us over. He informed us that we were speeding through a 60 mph zone. We pleaded innocent, saying we thought the speed limit on the entire turnpike was 70 mph. The officer said, "OK, I'm going to give you guys a warning ticket." Then, as he closed his book and turned to leave, he gave the first indication that he recognized us. He said, "By the way, I lost money on you guys again this year." I said, "How did you lose money? We just won the World Series." "Well," he said, "I bet on the Dodgers in 1947, 1949, 1952, and 1953. You guys lost every one. I said nuts to them this year, and I'm betting the Yankees." As Duke and I got in the car, Duke said, "Carl, we just met a born loser."

Magic in a Bottle

My two sons, Danny and Gary, often accompanied me to the Dodger clubhouse. They knew all of the Dodger players as friends and grew up with their kids. However, they watched the other New York teams, the Yankees and the Giants, on TV and were actually big fans of their baseball heroes, Mickey Mantle and Willie Mays.

My daughter, Susan, wasn't so fortunate in getting to hang around the clubhouse; however, when she was just a baby, she did get her share of baseball publicity.

During spring training, Betty brought the family to practice one day. I took a break and went over to see them. I took Susan and held her in my big Rawlings glove while I fed her from her bottle. Barney Stein, our photographer, took the picture on the next page. Once it ran in the paper, the Evenflo Baby Bottle Company recognized its bottle and signed us to a commercial using the picture. Susan made sports pages all over the country.

Clyde Wright

Baseball heroes aren't just admired by baseball fans. Those of us who were fortunate enough to play in the majors had our heroes, too. Some were former great players, and some were players we admired who were either teammates or opponents. To play with or against Jackie Robinson and not hold him in the highest esteem would be impossible. I also admired Sal Maglie and Allie Reynolds for their take-charge presence on the mound.

I went to a baseball function in New York and was checking in at the Commodore Hotel. As I walked toward the desk to register, I saw two baseball heroes coming toward me. They

The team photographer snapped me feeding my three-month-old daughter, Susan, as Betty, Danny, and Gary look on. *(Carl Erskine Collection)*

were two Yankee greats, Bill Dickey and Red Ruffing. As they came closer, Bill Dickey said, "Hello, Carl, how you doing? You know Red, here." We all shook hands and kept going. I couldn't believe I had just been put on a first-name basis with these two baseball greats of the past.

When I arrived at Yankee Stadium, I put on my Dodger uniform and went out to the visitors' dugout. It so happened that the Yankees were playing the California Angels that day, and out early and in the dugout was Clyde Wright, a fine left-handed pitcher. I had once seen him when Carson Newman College was a finalist in the NAIA World Series. At that time he was a hot prospect, and scouts were there en masse. I walked over to him and said, "Hello there, Clyde, good to see you. You're having a fine year." We shook hands and chatted. Then Clyde looked at me and said, "Man, I can't believe it when I hear a player like you call me by my first name." I said, "Clyde, let me tell you a story."

They'd Rather Be in Philly

There were several reasons opposing teams did not like coming to Ebbets Field. For one thing, we had a powerful team. But the atmosphere of Ebbets Field was one of intimidation. The raucous fans were quite close because there was very little foul territory. The fences were close, and our team always scored lots of runs. Then there was Hilda Chester, her cowbell, and her voice, which did not need a sound system to be heard. But the biggest annoyance was the five-piece ragtime band called "The Dodger Sym-phony."

Their classic routine, performed over and over again year after year, was done after an opponent made an out and was returning to the bench. The band would pick up his stride and in perfectly matched rhythm, step for step, would play "a rump de dump, a rump de dump" all the way to the dugout. If he slowed, the band slowed. If he sped up, which some did, the band would too. And then the finale was when he sat down—a huge KABOOM!

Players who had experienced this treatment before would often walk up and down in the dugout, refusing to sit down. They would fake it but never fool the sym-phony. They might go on for several minutes or half the inning, but when they finally sat down, KABOOM!

When you played at Ebbets Field, you just had to take it.

Dale Long

Every baseball player likes to please the crowd with his performance, but sometimes it's the wrong crowd in the wrong way. In 1956, Dale Long, a left-handed power hitter for the Pirates, had a home run streak of seven consecutive games, tying a National League record. The Dodgers opened the next series in Pittsburgh, and I was the starting pitcher. Forbes Field was packed to the rafters to see if Dale could get No. 8 and the new record.

The first time I faced him, he grounded out on my over-hand curve. The second time up, he hit the same pitch to deep right-center in the lower deck. The crowd went crazy. They cheered, threw cups, bats, and programs. Dale circled the bases; the roar was deafening. Bob Skinner, the next hitter, wouldn't get in the batter's box. We waited as the roar continued. When Dale stepped out of the dugout and tipped his cap, the cheers got even louder. Skinner still wouldn't get in the box. Eventually, the game went on. The Pirates won, and I had thrilled thousands of fans and hold the dubious record of being the victimized pitcher. Incidentally, Dale Long came to the big leagues as a left-handed catcher—later converted to first base.

The Safe Way Out

Ebbets Field was a small, intimate ballpark. The stands were very close to the field, and it was easy to hear the rabid Brooklyn fans yell at us on the field.

Fans at Ebbets often brought their lunch, and when they disapproved of an umpire's call or a player's rotten performance—look out!—here came the lunch! It was no secret that umpires and opposing players were intimidated by the sometimes wild, unruly fans of Ebbets Field.

It is a matter of record that in 1940, a seasoned umpire, George Magerkurth, umpiring at home plate, was attacked by a fan after a call went against the Dodgers. The Brooklyn fan pinned him to the ground and pummeled him until security hauled him away.

There's the incident during a Dodgers-Phillies game in which the umpire at second base, Beans Reardon, made a call on Granny Hamner sliding into the bag. Pee Wee Reese took the throw from Duke Snider and made the tag on a very close play. Reardon threw up his right hand, thumb in the air, and at the same time, yelled, "You're safe." Hamner, looking up, said, "Come on, Beans, am I out or safe?" Beans, remembering that he was at Ebbets Field, said, "Well, Granny, three of us here heard me call you safe; thirty-five thousand fans up there saw me call you out. Pal, you are out!"

Duke the Diplomat

In New York the Polo Grounds in Manhattan were about a 20-mile drive from Brooklyn. When we played the Giants there, it was easy for us to carpool. Duke, Pee Wee Reese, Rube Walker, and I lived in Bay Ridge, so we rode together, taking turns driving.

One day, Pee Wee picked us up for a night game at the Polo Grounds. We drove through the Battery Tunnel and up onto the Westside Highway. Almost immediately a motorcycle police officer pulled us over. As the policeman walked back to the car from his bike, Duke, seated in the front with Pee Wee, said, "OK, Pee Wee, let's see you do your stuff."

Pee Wee, always the gentleman, handed over his license. The officer looked at the license and said, "Where do you work, Mr. Reese?" Pee Wee said, "I work for the Dodgers." The officer reread the name on the license—Harold Henry Reese. Then a smile crossed his face. "Pee Wee!" he exclaimed. "Man, you're my favorite Dodger." Pee Wee said, "We're on our way to play the Giants. This is Duke Snider, Carl Erskine, and Rube Walker." The officer shook hands all around and wished us luck. And no ticket!

The next night Duke drove. As we passed through the Battery Tunnel and up onto the Westside Highway, sure enough, a different motorcycle police officer pulled us over. As he walked back to the car, Pee Wee said to Duke, "OK, big boy, let's see you do your stuff." When the officer reached our car, Duke thrust his license toward him and said, "I'm Duke Snider of the Dodgers, and this is Pee Wee Reese, Carl Erskine, and Rube Walker. We're on our way to the Polo Grounds to play the Giants." The officer looked down his nose at Duke and, with a snarl, said, "I don't like baseball." Duke growled back, "I don't like cops, either. Gimme that ticket!"

We rode the rest of the way to the Polo Grounds in total silence. We didn't dare give Duke the needle.

Sal the Barber

Sal Maglie was a real pro and a take-charge kind of pitcher. His curveball had the latest and sharpest break of any pitcher of his day.

A hug for no hits—Sal Maglie and I celebrate his domination of the Phillies in 1956. *(Carl Erskine Collection)*

He was especially tough on the Dodgers' heavy-hitting, right-handed lineup and was not bashful about throwing inside—inside the batting helmet, that is. Maglie relied heavily on his sharp curve; consequently, in order to be effective, he had to push the hitter back with fastballs inside—way inside.

Sal was known as a head hunter. The inside pitch he threw was described by former catcher and broadcaster Joe Garagiola as a "purpose" pitch. The purpose was to separate the head from the shoulders.

Actually, Sal was a real gentleman but a master of the brushback. His nickname, "The Barber," was given to him by Leo Durocher. Leo said, "He looked like the barber in the third chair at my barber shop." Throwing "close shaves" fit the name, too. Maglie had an 11-1 record at Ebbets Field and was 22-8 against us overall.

In 1956 Maglie was acquired by the Dodgers. He went 13-5 and tossed a no-hitter against the Phillies. Sal in a blue and white Dodger uniform, pitching on our side, was an unbelievable sight.

Captain Bassett

A real professional working his trade makes it look easy. Such was the case of a good friend, Captain Joe Bassett. Captain Bassett was a New York Harbor pilot and would bring the big liners in and out of the harbor. He was also a great Dodgers fan.

Following a night game at Ebbets Field, which we lost, he invited me to join him the next morning on board The Stockholm, a large luxury liner, as he took it out of the harbor. The next morning I was escorted to the bridge of The Stockholm, where Captain Bassett was positioned to maneuver the ship out to sea. The captain was a burly sailor with a salty vocabulary and a commanding presence. During World War II, he had been a naval advisor to General Eisenhower on D-Day landings and was a much decorated naval officer.

Captain Bassett was ready. From the bridge he could hand signal the seamen on the pier handling the huge mooring lines. He could also signal the tugs below with blasts from his whistle while speaking to the engine room through the intercom, giving commands for power as needed. A large crowd was watching from piers on either side.

As Captain Bassett routinely went about his task, he was barking at me with great emotion about last night's game. The big ship was slowly moving away from the pier. Bassett kept fuming about how Walter Alston had mismanaged the team into a loss. The Stockholm, however, made a flawless departure.

Decked

As long as baseball teams compete, there will, on occasion, be a brawl. During my minor league days in the Texas League, they had two unusual league rules: (1) hidden-ball tricks were not allowed, and (2) when a fight started on the field, umpires, security guards, and officials were to step aside and let the fight run its course. In that league, if you started a fight, you had to want to finish it.

In the big leagues, more control is exercised; however, fights do occur from time to time. The best punch I ever saw thrown in the ring or out was at Ebbets Field in a night game against Cincinnati. A Cincinnati relief pitcher named Raul Sanchez had a reputation for throwing at hitters. In an earlier series in Cincinnati, he had drilled Jim Gilliam in the ribs. Jim was a quiet, even-tempered person, but he did have a good memory. When Jim came to bat against Sanchez at Ebbets, he laid down a drag bunt toward first base, drawing Sanchez to the line to field it. Jim then jumped Sanchez and pinned him to the ground. Both benches emptied. Out of the Cincy dugout came tough ex-Marine Don Hoak, his eyes ever glued on Gilliam pounding away at Sanchez. What he didn't see was our man Charlie Neal, who had singled out Hoak. Neal hit Hoak a clean right-handed punch to the chin. Hoak reeled backward and fell over the mound. By then, security was on the scene and the fight was over. All parties involved were ejected and subsequently fined.

The National League's headquarters happened to be in Cincinnati, so during our next trip there, the league president, Warren Giles, had Hoak and Neal come to his office, accompanied by the clubs' respective player representatives. Ted Kluszewski represented the Reds, and I represented the Dodgers.

After a stern warning by President Giles, he asked Hoak and Neal to shake hands and forget the incident. Reluctantly, the two reached out to shake. Hoak said, "I'll shake, but I ain't gonna forget it." Neither will any of the rest of us who saw Neal's punch.

Belated

One of the emptiest feelings a person can have is to neglect to say thank you to someone and then find out it's too late and you can't. This has happened to me twice in my baseball career.

As a minor league pitcher, I was approached at the end of the season by Jack Onslow, manager of the Waterloo, Iowa, White Sox. He told me I was tipping off my curve and they were calling my pitches. He told me I'd have real trouble in a higher classification, and he helped me see how to correct my fault. I did correct it and was moved quickly to the big leagues the next season. The change in my curveball made the difference, and it became my money pitch.

Jack went on to manage in the big leagues with the Chicago White Sox. I never did see him again, nor did I ever thank him after I made it to the majors. He died in 1960.

Al Scheunemann had been a trainer in the Dodger organization. In time he became the trainer for the Chicago Cubs. I was having arm miseries in May 1956. From my hotel room in Chicago, I called Al Scheunemann. I had visited our own club trainer, Dr. Harold Wendler, so many times that I was embarrassed to go to him again.

Al said, "Stay right there, I'm coming to see you." He checked my shoulder and found a knot the size of a golf ball. He said, "Come with me to see our club doctor." This was a highly unusual practice, but I was desperate. The doctor gave me a deep shot of cortisone and told me I would be sore for a couple of days. Little did he know that I was pitching the next day in Brooklyn.

The next day—Saturday, May 12, 1956—I faced the New York Giants at Ebbets Field. Final score: Dodgers 3, Giants 0. They also got zero hits. Al Scheunemann, thanks—wherever you are.

Jackie and Sheehan

One of the most intense players of any era was Jackie Robinson. During the nine seasons I was Jackie's teammate, I watched how one man changed the face of baseball and advanced the cause of social justice even more so, I believe, than Martin Luther King Jr.

During his final season, he had begun to gray, had picked up a little weight, and had physically slowed down. However, his competitive drive had not diminished. Because he was so often quoted and misquoted, Jackie never missed reading any edition of the seven New York newspapers. Consequently, he saw the article quoting Tom Sheehan, chief New York Giants scout, who said, "The Dodgers are over the hill. Jackie's too old, Campy's too old and Erskine, he can't win with the garbage he's been throwing up there."

I also read that article that Saturday, May 12, 1956, and it hurt, because I was having severe arm problems but was scheduled to pitch that afternoon at Ebbets Field against the Giants. My spirits were low, and I literally had nothing going for me but a prayer.

The game started, and the opposing pitcher was Al Worthington. I got through inning one, then two, three, and four. In the fifth, Willie Mays hit a shot to Jackie's left at third base. Jackie made a marvelous clean pickup of the smash on one hop and threw Willie out easily. Through six innings, no score. Finally, we scored three runs in the seventh. I breezed through the eighth, and when Alvin Dark hit a one-hopper back to me with two out in the ninth, I had miraculously pitched a no-hit, no-run game—thanks to Jackie.

Jackie rushed to the mound, shook my hand, and then turned and raced toward the Giants' dugout, where Tom Sheehan was seated. Jackie reached in the hip pocket of his Dodger uniform, pulled the clipping out, waved it at Sheehan, and shouted, "How do you like that garbage?" That was Jackie, a fierce competitor.

A Pressing Situation

Baseball wives have as much to learn as their husbands about baseball. For instance, keeping score is often done in the stands by the wives marking their scorecards. Once, my wife, Betty, was sitting next to other wives and keeping score. One wife took exception to how Betty had just scored her husband. For that time at bat, Betty marked "P.U." The offended wife relaxed when Betty said that "P.U." meant "Pop Up."

Campy, Jackie, and I celebrate after the last out of my no-hitter against the Giants in 1956. *(Carl Erskine Collection)*

Although baseball players are trying to raise their batting averages and pitchers are trying to lower their earned run averages, baseball wives are busy trying to raise their kids and do their chores at home. However, that doesn't exempt a baseball wife from the frayed nerves and anxious moments of the game.

On May 12, 1956, I was pitching against the New York Giants. Betty was at home, ironing and listening to the game. The first inning went okay for me, as did the second, the third, and the fourth. Betty was ironing a tablecloth and was reluctant to finish it because she feared that might just change my luck. So she continued to iron the tablecloth, turning it over. The fifth, sixth, and seventh innings went fine, too. The ironing continued. When I retired Alvin Dark in the ninth to end the game, Betty finally quit ironing the tablecloth. I had allowed no hits or runs; she had not scorched a spot. That's teamwork.

The Old Hometown

I have lived in Anderson, Indiana, since I was born December 13, 1926. I am truly linked to my hometown—both as an Anderson Indians basketball player performing in our famous gymnasium, The Wigwam, and as a high school baseball pitcher, where I got my first uniform as a freshman. When major league scouts started following me, my horizons expanded.

Baseball took me around the world, but I always maintained my permanent home in Anderson.

Throughout my career, my wife, Betty, kept one scrapbook containing only telegrams. These wires came principally from boosters back home. Most of them congratulated me on big victories or wished me well before an important start, say, in the World Series. I could always count on my old coach, Charlie Cummings, to send me a telegram when I lost. He knew I needed one then.

The biggest boost I got from my hometown resulted from a game I pitched on May 12, 1956. It was the Game of the Week on national TV with famed announcers Dizzy Dean and Buddy Blatner. All during the game, they kept referring to Anderson, Indiana. The mayor of Anderson and the chamber of commerce were ecstatic to get such great national exposure. When this game turned out to be a no-hit, no-run game—the first ever on national television—they really went wild.

The following day, I read in a New York paper a quote from Mayor Ralph Ferguson saying that Anderson was going to have a big day when I came home and that the town was going to give me a white Cadillac. In fact, that is what happened when I returned in October.

There was a parade, a Little League game, and finally, a big banquet held in the YMCA gym. The keys to a 1957 white Cadillac were presented to Betty and me.

Some of my Dodger teammates used to kid me and say, "Somebody ruined a good Indiana farm when they built Anderson." I say, "Everybody should have a hometown like Anderson."

Thanks, Mickey

Mickey Mantle had it all, including those All-American-boy good looks. Never was there a player so gifted in so many ways. Only injuries kept him from achieving even more amazing stats than he did.

I faced Mantle in four different World Series and was in awe of his power, speed, and overall ability. He was a free swinger and struck out a lot, but he always took his best cut.

In the 1956 World Series in Yankee Stadium, Mantle surprised me by laying down a bunt, even though I had two strikes on him. I thought this was a stupid play and that he didn't

This brand-new Cadillac was a hometown gift to me and my family. *(Carl Erskine Collection)*

know the count. I even thought that if I were his manager, I'd certainly fine him for bunting with two strikes.

Years later at an Old-Timers' Game at Yankee Stadium, I was visiting with Whitey Ford, Vic Raschi, Hank Bauer, and Billy Martin. I asked them how smart a player Mantle was. They said he was a heads-up ballplayer. When I mentioned the bunt, they all began to laugh. They said, "Oh, he knew the count, all right, and told us, 'If Erskine gets two strikes on me, I know he'll throw that nasty overhand curve, and I'm going to bunt that so-and-so.'"

My curveball never received a greater compliment.

Perfectly Awful

On October 8, 1956, the sun rose as always, but there was never a day like this one—before or after.

Sal Maglie, starting pitcher for the Dodgers, and Don Larsen, starting pitcher for the Yankees, faced each other in a World Series game at Yankee Stadium. About the sixth inning, we were trailing, 2-0, and someone on the Dodger bench said, "You know, we haven't had a base runner yet." That woke us up, and we watched intently as Don Larsen continued to deny us a base runner. Finally, he struck out pinch hitter Dale Mitchell to record his 27th consecutive out for the first and only perfect game in World Series history.

Japan

In 1956 the Dodgers made a five-week postseason tour of Japan. We drew great crowds and found Japanese baseball to be very respectable. In fact, we lost to the Tokyo Giants, and Walter O'Malley was very upset with the team. He was embarrassed. He held a team meeting and read the riot act. He said,

This photo was given to me by the Mick himself. *(Courtesy of Mickey Mantle)*

"I know this is a goodwill tour, and I want you to be gentlemen. Sign autographs and be cordial. However, when you put on that Dodger uniform, I want you to remember Pearl Harbor."

There was evidence that Western culture was beginning to show up in Japan in the way of fashion, music, and certain customs. Duke Snider, Roy Campanella, and I were asked to endorse Canon camera equipment. The deal was to run during our tour, and we were to be paid in Canon equipment. We went to the Canon factory and were allowed to pick out whatever and as much as we liked. There were several pictures taken of the three of us, and we all selected the cameras and accessories we wanted.

Within a few days, as we shopped with our wives in a Tokyo department store, we began to see these life-size stand-up cutouts of the three of us. There we were in full Dodger uniforms, in living color, each holding a Canon camera and each of us with a slight slant to our eyes. Campy looked like a sumo wrestler.

Hometown

In baseball, a major league player is often linked to his hometown. My hometown of Anderson, Indiana, followed me all around baseball and still does to this day, decades after I retired from the game.

My roommate, Duke Snider, was always amazed at how many times someone would come to the dugout and say— and this happened in cities all around the majors—"Where's Erskine? I'm from Anderson, Indiana."

When I visited Duke in California on my first trip there, he showed me the town. Returning from a theater late one night in Hollywood, while crossing a deserted street, a lone car whizzed by. Out of the window a voice yelled, "Hey Erskine, how you doin'? I'm from Anderson." When Duke moved to

Campy, Duke, and I focus in on the action at the baseball stadium in Tokyo, Japan. *(Carl Erskine Collection)*

Fallbrook, California, and stopped at the post office to register his new address, the postmaster told him that he was from Anderson. Duke was amazed.

On a goodwill tour of Japan with the Dodgers and at the ballpark in Osaka, a fellow came to the dugout and asked for Erskine. Duke said, "Don't tell me, don't tell me you're from Anderson, Indiana." "Yes," said Roger Whitehead, a friend of mine who was stationed there in the army. Flabbergasted, Duke remarked, "Nobody lives in Anderson, Indiana. They are all somewhere else."

In 2003 I sold my farm and built a new house in Anderson. I wrote Duke, who lives in Fallbrook, California, and gave him my new address: on Fallbrook Lane. I guess Duke gets to have the last laugh after all.

Close Call

One off season I was driving to Cincinnati and made a wrong turn, causing me to end up on a county road north of the city. Soon I arrived in Darrtown, Ohio, where Walt Alston lived. There was only one store/gas station and a phone booth. That was the whole town. I stopped at the phone booth and looked at the skinny little phone book for Walt's number. When I dialed it, Walt answered. I said, "Hello, Skipper. I'm passing through town and wanted to stop and say hello. Tell me where you live." He said, "Turn around. I'm watching you out of the kitchen window."

Sandy's Reply*

It was a hot night in Miami, and the bus the Dodgers were riding in to go back to the McAllister Hotel was an unair-conditioned, hard ride. The mood was sour because we had just taken a sound beating from the Braves at Miami Stadium. Even though it was just a spring training game, losing was not taken lightly.

Miami is crisscrossed with train tracks, and so sure enough we were stopped by a very slow-moving train. As we sat there waiting in the dark, the combination of the heat, the humidity, and a poorly played game made the troops very restless. After several minutes, one of our coaches, Billy Herman, could take it no longer.

"You can give this town back to the Jews," he shouted.

Oh boy, everyone on the bus cringed. Sitting just across the aisle was a young, left-handed pitcher named Sandy Koufax. He was Jewish, and he was always a gentleman, ready to defuse any hint of anti-Semitism that he encountered in the league.

He just sat there in silence. The only sound was the passing of the train. Then, out of the dark, his soft voice said, "Now, Billy, you know we already have it."

The tension broke as the team erupted in laughter. Sandy had proven to be bigger than the moment.

*At the risk of writing a compromising story, I contacted Sandy Koufax to request his permission to tell it and to have him check the details for accuracy. Sandy said he remembered the incident very well.

A 1957 win at Ebbets Field is cause for Johnny Podres, me, and Sandy Koufax to celebrate. *(Carl Erskine Collection)*

Hen House

D on Demeter was a solid major league outfielder for the Dodgers, both in Brooklyn and in Los Angeles. He was very even-tempered and dedicated to his church.

Don was as intense as any other good professional, but he never used any profanity. That is, he never used the conventional words. Instead, when he was upset over a bad call, he would say, "That 'hen house' umpire called that 'hen house' pitch a strike when that 'hen house' pitch was a foot outside."

'Scuse Me?

A fter I lost a tough night game at Ebbets Field, I was looking forward to the off day that followed. A good friend, Captain Joe Dowd, had invited me to go fishing at Sheepshead Bay. I rose early, well before daylight, and hailed a cab to go after Captain Dowd.

As we rode along, the cabbie asked me if I had seen the game last night. I said, "As a matter of fact, I did." "Well," he said, "I could tell Oiskin' was gonna have trouble. I woulda yanked him in the third inning." I said, "They only had one run off him by the third inning." "Yeah," he said, "but I watched this guy before—Alston shoulda pulled him." This chat continued for several blocks until we arrived at 404 Caton Avenue, Captain Dowd's address. When I went to the door, I told the captain about the cabbie and said, "Let's have some fun." All the way to Sheepshead Bay, the captain sided with the cabbie in really working me over.

When we arrived at the dock, I told Captain Dowd that I would take the fishing tackle over by a streetlight and asked him to take my $20 bill and pay the cabbie—and also tell the cabbie who had been in the taxi with him.

In a couple of minutes I saw the cabbie's head pop up from the other side of the cab. He stared at me and then came hurrying around behind the cab with his right hand extended. He said, "Oisk, Oisk! You're beautiful. It's that Alston I can't stand."

A Ball in the Hand Is Worth Two

Baseball rules have stayed basically the same for decades, but occasionally, something happens to cause the rules committee to alter or change a rule.

The rules state that a base runner, if hit by a batted ball between the bases, is out, and the batter is credited with a hit.

Situation: Ebbets Field. Don Hoak on second, Jim Gilliam on first. As Hoak leads off second, the batter hits a routine grounder toward the shortstop. This is a cinch double play ball. Hoak, the base runner, steps to his right and fields the ball bare-handed, then drops it. Of course, he is out, but he avoided the double play. The rule now reads that should this happen again, both the runner and the batter are out.

Taxed

Gil Hodges and I used the same tax accountant in Brooklyn. Herman Kaplan was a sharp dresser and a tax expert of major league caliber.

One day, Herman called to tell me that the Internal Revenue Service had asked for an audit on two of my tax returns, 1952 and 1953. He asked me to provide him with the records he needed and said he would appear on my behalf at the IRS office.

Several weeks passed and Herman called me again. He said, "Well, I met with the IRS on your behalf today, and by the way, how many no-hitters have you pitched?" I was confused by the questions, but I answered, "Two." "Well," he said, "I did the equivalent of that today. I got the IRS to accept those two years, 1952 and 1953, as submitted. You're home free."

"Steeee-rike!"

The world knows that Jackie Robinson was the first black player in the major leagues. However, most people may not remember that the first black umpire was Emmett Ashford.

There's the classic story of Emmett being challenged at home plate for calling a strike on a half-swing. When the manager charged him and argued that it wasn't a strike, Emmett stood his ground. Finally, the manager insisted that Ashford check the call with the first base umpire, who may have seen the swing better. Emmett obliged and walked to first base to confer with his partner. In a few moments, Emmett came back to home plate. He told the manager, "Yes, it was a strike. Now you have it in black and white."

The Little Colonel

Captain Harold Henry "Pee Wee" Reese wore No. 1 on the back of his uniform. There's something very symbolic about that. For example, whenever the manager wanted a player's input, he would always go to Pee Wee first. Reese was the central figure in supporting Jackie Robinson as the first black player in baseball. Duke Snider named him first when he declared that Pee Wee was the greatest Dodger of them all. And the kids at Ebbets Field picked Pee Wee time and again as their first choice on *The Happy Felton Knothole Gang* TV show.

In spite of all his great hustle on the field, Pee Wee was one of the slowest players to get dressed and leave the clubhouse. He would sit in his captain's chair in front of his locker, read the paper, smoke his pipe, and ignore the world. When the rest of us who rode with Pee Wee would tell him to hurry up, he would say, "When you hurry in and out of the clubhouse, you hurry in and out of baseball."

Pee Wee didn't hurry. He had 19 years of major league service (three in the military), a long broadcasting career in baseball, and represented Louisville Slugger bats, which are made by Hillerich & Bradsby, to major league teams until his retirement.

Pee Wee got his name as a kid because he won a marbles championship in Kentucky. He could hit the smallest marbles, which were called peewees.

When Pee Wee passed away from cancer at age 81, one newspaper story summed up his significance to the Dodgers— and to baseball in general: "This Pee Wee was a giant."

A Branch with Deep Roots

Branch Rickey was a multitalented man. He could have been a businessman, politician, a preacher, or an actor. In the late 1950s he became all rolled into one on a soundstage in Hollywood. Mr. Rickey was a part of the Fellowship of Christian Athletes, an organization still in its infancy, and FCA executives decided to create a movie to give the group more exposure.

The cast was selected and met in Hollywood for the filming: Dr. Louis Evans, a powerful Presbyterian minister; Rafer Johnson, a student at UCLA and an Olympic gold medal winner in the decathlon; Mr. Rickey, as one of the founders of FCA; and me. As we waited in the studio, the director was very nervous. He had a bunch of amateurs who were supposed to know their lines, make the right gestures, and therefore be good actors. To add to his anxiety, the main actor in the film—Mr. Rickey, who was flying overnight from Pittsburgh—was late.

Finally Mr. Rickey and his party rushed in. The director greeted Mr. Rickey very nervously and said, "I know this will be very hard for you, and you have some extensive dialogue." "Oh yes," Mr. Rickey stated. "I've been studying the script, and I've made a few changes." That made the director even more nervous. "We should have a dry run, and because of the length of your dialogue, we should do it in small parts."

We were seated on a davenport in the middle of the stage. I was to lead Mr. Rickey into his lines. I said, "Mr. Rickey, during our first interview, you asked me a question I did not expect to hear: 'Young man, do you go to church?'" Mr. Rickey began in his halting and slow-paced delivery, "Well, I ask that question to every young man I signed." He then continued with feeling, raising his voice for emphasis and quieting it for reflection and gesturing where appropriate. He continued on powerfully through the entire script. He was spellbinding. When he finished, the light crew, cameramen, and stagehands began to applaud—but the director was about to collapse. He said, "Oh my, we should have filmed that. He can never do that again."

With apprehension, he set up the crew to roll film this time. I did my short lead-in, and Mr. Rickey started. Not only did he deliver a perfect monologue again, but he gave it with even greater power. This time the whole studio gave him a standing ovation, full of bravos. One of the cameramen said that he had filmed John Barrymore, the great actor, and that Mr. Rickey's performance was every bit in the same class.

As for Mr. Rickey, he grabbed his coat and hat and left as quickly as he had come. He said he had meetings back in Pittsburgh. But what he left behind both then and now is his impact for good that still lasts even after his death in 1965.

"Luck," he said, "is the residue of design." Mr. Rickey's hidden talents planted roots that continue to bear fruit to this day.

P.S. Mr. Rickey had a son, Branch Jr. We called him "The Twig."

Buzzie on Passes

Our last year in Brooklyn was 1957, and we weren't playing very well. Jackie had retired, and the fans already knew the Dodgers were moving to L.A. The season's attendance was spotty. I was player representative, so I got a call one night before game time from our general manager, Buzzie Bavasi. He was really upset because there were more than 70 passes requested by the players on the pass list that night. He said to me, "Who are all these people?" I said, "They must be friends of the players." Buzzie replied, "The way you guys are playing, you don't have that many friends."

Erskine Plays Center Field

My son Danny made a Brooklyn Little League team when he was seven. He came home with this uniform after tryouts, and I thought the coach probably just favored Danny because he was the son of a Brooklyn Dodger. The coach said, "This kid earned that uniform. He catches fly balls better than anybody I've got." Even though Danny was a well developed boy at age seven, the uniform sponsor's name went around him twice: "Ninety-Second Street Car Wash."

In 1957 it was announced that the Dodgers would be leaving Brooklyn for Los Angeles in 1958. It was a common

Danny and me at Ebbets Field. *(Carl Erskine Collection)*

occurrence to be stopped on the street or called on the phone by Brooklyn fans bemoaning the fact that the Dodgers were leaving. "We'll miss you guys. No more games at Ebbets?" and on and on. I spoke with Danny's coach, and he, too, was crying the blues because the team was moving. Of course, I assumed he was expressing the same disappointment of all these other fans. Not so. He said, "This is a tough thing to handle; I'm really depressed. I'm going to lose the best center fielder in the league."

Horse Face

The rivalry between the Brooklyn Dodgers and the New York Giants was so intense that it defies description. With three major league teams in New York, most family loyalties were split at least two, sometimes three, ways. The fact that the Giants were in the National League meant we faced them 22 times each season—11 at Ebbets, 11 at the Polo Grounds.

Duke Snider, my roommate, played center field and was the target of Giants fans who sat in the outfield bleachers at the Polo Grounds. One man in particular really got to Duke. He constantly called him "horse face." Duke would become furious as this guy continued to needle him. This verbal harassment went on for several seasons, until baseball's West Coast expansion in 1958 required us to open the season in San Francisco at Seals Stadium.

Our team bus pulled up to the stadium, and the many waiting fans were held back by barricades so that we could get to the clubhouse. As we stepped off the bus, here's this same Giants fan, and he yells, "Hey, horse face, you thought you got rid of me, didn't you?" Even Duke had to shake his head and smile—that great rivalry moved west, too.

Matt Brinduse

Opening day in Los Angeles in 1958 was a historic event. It marked the first ever major league game in that city, and nearly 80,000 fans were on hand at Memorial Coliseum to witness it.

Being new to L.A., I didn't really know anyone except a friend, Matt Brinduse, from Anderson, Indiana, who now lived in Long Beach and drove a delivery truck for a laundry. I called Matt and asked him if he wanted tickets to the ballgame. He was very excited to get to attend.

Of course, on game day I was too busy with the job at hand and never saw Matt. We did beat the Giants in a rather wild game for the first win in Los Angeles. Following the game, our manager, Walt Alston, held a press conference.

The press room was filled with writers, photographers, and radio and TV people, all more or less strangers to Walt. The questions began, and Walt fielded them one by one. A voice in the back said, "Mr. Alston, Erskine pitched a great game today, didn't he?" Walt said, "Yes, Carl did a good job for us." Several more questions, then the voice in the rear said, "Mr. Alston, Erskine is one of the best pitchers you've ever had, right?" "Well," said Alston, "Carl's been a productive pitcher all along." A few more questions, then again, this voice from the back: "Mr. Alston, wouldn't you say Carl's your ace?" Walt turned to Lee Scott, our traveling secretary, and said, "Who the hell is that?" Of course, Lee didn't know that it was Matt Brinduse, the laundry man from Long Beach and my pass for opening day.

L.A. Movie Stars

Those of us who were transitional players (i.e., we played in both Brooklyn and Los Angeles) had to make quite an adjustment from Ebbets Field to the Memorial

Coliseum in L.A. The Dodgers played there for three seasons while Dodger Stadium was being built.

It wasn't unusual to be on the mound during a game and look over at the dugout to see several players looking back over the edge, into the stands, to see Lana Turner, Danny Kaye, Jeff Chandler, and other famous Hollywood movie stars attending the game.

"Kids Say the Darndest Things"

When the Dodgers moved to California in 1958, it marked a historic time for baseball. Major league baseball was on the West Coast for the first time. We were interviewed, our wives were interviewed, even our children were interviewed. Art Linkletter had my son Danny on his TV show called *Kids Say the Darndest Things*. Danny was nine years old.

The Dodgers had gotten off to a slow start that season, and we weren't winning like the great teams of the Brooklyn era. Art asked Danny where his dad worked. Danny said, "Oh, he doesn't work, he plays for the Dodgers." Art said, "Oh, yes, the team just moved here from Brooklyn. Danny, do you know what the letters on the Dodger cap stand for now? What does L.A. stand for?" Danny replied, "Lost Again."

Campy

Inspiration is impossible to measure, but when it hits, ordinary people do some remarkably extraordinary things.

In 1958 I began my 13th season as a pitcher in the Dodger organization. I was passed the age of 30 and had battled an arm injury for most of those years. I was tired physically and mentally. The Dodgers were doing all they could to keep me going, but time for me was running out.

One of my unpleasant treatments was to go to a hospital either at home or on the road once a week and get a deep injection of cortisone in my right shoulder. I had won a couple of games, including the opener in Los Angeles, but I was struggling. My catcher, Roy Campanella, had been severely injured in an auto accident just before spring training, and rookie Johnny Roseboro was sharing the catching with Rube Walker.

On our first trip into Philadelphia, I took the train to New York to visit Campy. I happened to be the first team member to visit him after his accident. Roy and I couldn't speak for about five minutes. He was strapped face-down in a special bed and could only move his head and eyes. I know when he saw me, he saw the whole team. That was a tough five minutes. Then we talked. He was so positive, so enthusiastic about his therapy and his hope for recovery. He also said he watched games on TV using a special TV set and mirrors so he could see looking face-down. He told me he'd be watching me pitch against the Phillies the next night.

I rode back to Philly on the train and was deeply moved, thinking about Roy. The next night he was strong on my mind as I warmed up. Then during the game, with almost every pitch, I could visualize Roy in that bed, watching me, pulling for us to win. We did, 2-1. It was the last complete game I ever pitched in the majors.

Who's on First?

One of the best comedy teams of all times was Abbott and Costello. Their famous routine of "Who's on First?" is enshrined at Cooperstown as a piece of baseball history. Bud Abbott was a regular at the ballpark in Los

Don Zimmer and I celebrate a 2-1 victory over the Philadelphia Phillies. I threw my last complete game, and Zimmer knocked in the winning run. *(Carl Erskine Collection)*

Angeles and gave all of us with the Dodgers a recording of their famous script.

In the routine, Abbott says he has a baseball team, and since players in baseball have funny nicknames like Dizzy, Daffy, etc., his team has unusual names, too. "Who's" on first, "What's" on second, and "I Don't Know" is on third.

Lou Costello asks Abbott "Who's on first?" Abbott says, "Yes." "Who's the first baseman?" asks Costello. "Yes," says Abbott. Costello says, "I want to know who's playing first base." "Yes, he is," says Abbott. "Now, look," says Costello, "do you pay those players?" "Oh, sure," says Abbott. "Well, when the first baseman comes in for his pay, who gets the money?" "Yes, he does—every dime of it. In fact, sometimes even his wife comes in for his pay." "Whose wife?" asks Costello. "Yes," says Abbott. This routine is rapid-fire and goes on and on for each position.

America so embraced this crazy baseball routine that we often hear in business meetings or private conversations when something is in question . . . "Who's on first?"

Rube Squatting

I n spring training at Dodgertown in 1959, it had been announced that Ebbets Field was going to be demolished. Some of the writers were asking the players their reaction to the demise of the famous old ballpark. Pee Wee Reese said, "Well, they won't have any trouble with the outfield walls because Pete Reiser has softened them up." (In fact, Pete and his numerous collisions with the walls had prompted the placement of the padding on those fences.) Carl Furillo wondered what would happen to the Abe Stark sign under the right field scoreboard that he guarded for so long. (Abe offered a suit to anyone who could hit a baseball off his sign.) Rube Walker, our backup catcher who saw most of his action warming up pitchers because

These baseball-like wrecking balls brought down the Brooklyn Dodgers' old home, Ebbets Field, in 1959. *(Carl Erskine Collection)*

Campy caught almost every game, asked what was going to be put in place of Ebbets Field. When told it would be a 50-story apartment building, Rube said, "I wonder who'll be squatting where I used to squat."

Throw over Screen

W e've all had the experience of wishing we had responded with a word or action after it's too late. This happened to me during a night game in 1959 in the Memorial Coliseum while I was pitching against the Cubs. This stadium, improvised for baseball, was oval-shaped, so the left field foul pole was only 250 feet from home plate. It had a high screen, but pop flies could go over it. Even I used to hit home runs there in batting practice.

This was late in my career. I was battling a bad arm, and I needed every break I could get. In the top of the ninth, we were leading, 3-2. With two out and a man on, Chuck Tanner came in to pinch hit. With two strikes and a ball on him, I jammed him with a high, inside pitch. He blooped it down the left field line just inches inside the foul pole for a two-run homer. As I stood there while he circled the bases, I glared at that fence.

When the umpire threw me a new ball, my first instinct was to fire it over that 250-foot screen to show the world how short it was. That probably would have been remembered more than Tanner's bloop home run. I still dream of throwing the baseball over that short fence from the mound.

Fan-tastic

F an mail is one of the biggest dividends a player can earn as a result of his baseball career. Kids are great, and some of their letters are right on target:

"Dear Mr. Erskine, I didn't see you pitch but my grandfather did."

"Dear Mr. Erskine, Please send me your autograph and could you tell me how to throw a spitball?"

"Dear Mr. Erskine, I'm not writing for your autograph but here's mine on my Little League picture."

I once received a fan letter from Scotland, where the name Erskine is rather common. The fan said, "We must be related. You look just like Uncle Willie."

The most flattering note was a birth announcement from Los Angeles announcing the birth of Carl Erskine Gibson. A year later, I received a picture of a really cute little boy.

The most unique letters came from John Hildebrand, a missionary in South Africa. We corresponded from the 1950s until his death in 1998. I would get a letter in August, and he would be two months behind in congratulating me on a win in June.

The fan letters I got from Japan included newspaper clippings, but I couldn't read them.

An architect in Wisconsin wrote me and called me often. He wanted the architectural plans for Ebbets Field. I told him I had no idea where to find them. He then asked me to describe it in great detail. I told him I only saw it from the mound.

Geisha Boy

After visiting Japan in 1956, the Dodgers were a natural to be invited by Jerry Lewis to be in his movie *Geisha Boy*. We filmed it in Hollywood at the old ballpark used in the Pacific Coast League days.

We made $300 each in a deal I negotiated with Jerry Lewis because I was the player representative. Although he used only some of the Dodgers, Lewis agreed to pay everyone on the roster the same. My pitch to him was that if this group represented the Dodgers, then the whole team should be paid. He agreed. I personally never had an agent. Now I am one.

Pop-Ups

There are many special skills used in baseball. Some of them are rarely seen by the fans because they are in evidence only before game time. One of these skills involves hitting fungoes. A fungo bat is longer, thinner, and lighter than a regular wooden bat and is used to hit fly balls for outfield and infield practice. This assignment is usually given to a coach or a pitcher. A fungo bat in the hands of a skilled fungo hitter is something to see. Good fungo hitters are extremely accurate, placing routine fly balls, line drives, and towering fly balls that challenge even seasoned outfielders.

One such skillful fungo hitter was Ed Roebuck, a good relief pitcher for the Dodgers during the 1950s. Ed could hit the ball higher and farther than anyone in baseball at that time. Now this may not seem like a marketable skill, but when you're the best at something, it usually earns you an opportunity to do something special.

In 1964, when Judge Roy Hofheinz in Houston, Texas, was planning the first ever domed stadium, there was a question as to how high it should be built to assure that a major league fly ball could not reach the top of the superstructure. So who got the call? Ed Roebuck.

Walter O'Malley, owner of the Dodgers, was acquainted with the architect designing the Astrodome and suggested that Ed Roebuck could help find the answer. Using a supply of new baseballs, Ed hit towering fly balls that were measured by transit and timed by a stopwatch. Calculations were then made of their height. The plans were drawn accordingly. Incidentally, a batted ball never reached the superstructure in the Astrodome.

Oh, yes. Ed Roebuck had once been fined $75 by manager Walt Alston for hitting fungoes out of the Los Angeles Coliseum. Walter O'Malley repaid Ed the $75 for his performance.

'Round About

The only time I ever got chewed out royally by my manager was in Los Angeles during my last year in pro baseball. I had battled an injured pitching arm for several seasons, and the misery was still with me. I had learned to live with it.

One day Don Drysdale brought a boomerang to the ballpark. We had it in the outfield during batting practice. None of us could make it complete the circle and come all the way back; however, I was having the best throws, and on each one of my tosses, it got closer. Walt Alston came out and saw me throwing that boomerang. (We were in fifth place at the time.) He read me the riot act and confiscated the boomerang.

My Contribution

In 1959 the Los Angeles Boys of Summer were into late autumn or early winter. By June 15, we were in fifth place and going nowhere. That prompted me to retire voluntarily and become a coach. At this time the Dodgers reached into their minor leagues and made some major changes. Roger Craig replaced me; Maury Wills became the shortstop. Frank Howard, Larry Sherry, and Chuck Essegian were added to the roster. By August, the team began to move. In September, the Dodgers tied the league-leading Milwaukee Braves, beat them in a playoff, and then defeated the Chicago White Sox for the first World Series win in Los Angeles.

The Dodger players voted me a half-share of the World Series winnings. Not because I won any games, but because when I retired, Roger Craig won 11 games in my place.

Once in a Lifetime

In my 14 years in professional baseball, I have seen thousands of innings. I actually pitched in about 2,000 innings. During that much baseball, you would think one would have encountered virtually every possibility. Here are three that I'll bet happened only once:

1. Duke Snider, batting in Sportsman's Park in St. Louis, hit a long drive to right center field. The ball struck a clock mounted on a light standard atop the stands for a home run. The clock was a Longines and had the name in neon under the clock. Duke's drive knocked out the letters L-O-N-G. The next night Duke again hit a towering drive to right center. Yes, the ball hit the same clock, just missing by inches the remaining lighted neon letters. When the Longines people heard about this, they sent Duke and his wife, Beverly, each a fine Longines watch.

2. At Ebbets Field the scoreboard was inside the playing field. The ground rules stated that "any ball staying on the scoreboard" (318 feet from home plate) was a home run. On the face of the scoreboard was a Schaefer beer sign. The "h" and the first "e" in Schaefer were outlined in neon to flash "hit" or "error" by the official scorer.

Hank Thompson, third baseman for the New York Giants, hit a line drive off me that hit the "h" in Schaefer and stuck. Carl Furillo, playing in right field, tried to jar the ball loose. It stayed stuck in full view, 20 feet up, on the face of the scoreboard. Thompson went all the way around the bases and scored. After a long argument, the rule was applied ("any ball staying on the scoreboard . . ."), and the hit was declared a home run. The game was delayed while the grounds crew put up a long ladder to retrieve the ball.

3. Milwaukee County Stadium originally had a chain-link fence around the outfield. Billy Bruton, a speedy left-handed-hitting outfielder for the Milwaukee Braves, hit a line drive into right center field. The ball hit the fence and dropped straight down.

Duke Snider, playing center field for the Dodgers, and Carl Furillo, playing right field, both converged on the spot where the ball dropped. Bruton was speeding toward second base. Snider and Furillo both plunged their hands into the grass at the base of the fence. Each came up with a baseball and each turned and fired to second base—two balls in play! Bruton was safe, but it took several minutes for the umpires to decide that one ball was a batting practice ball left unnoticed when the game started.

From a Different Dugout

When I left baseball in 1960, I had to find a new way to make a living because I had four kids at home. I decided to enroll in Anderson College, a small school in my hometown. I needed a refresher course to get my mind ready for the business world, so I took math, accounting, and English as part of my transition. But I met reality when I walked into my first class at 7:00 a.m. as a 32-year-old freshman. The class got very quiet—they thought I was there to teach the class.

Because I was a student, the athletic department asked me to coach their baseball team for one year while they searched for a permanent coach. Because I had had baseball in my head for 14 years while I was in the majors, I agreed to do it even though the uniforms were orange and black, the Giants' colors.

Now a player knows most of the general rules of baseball, but I got some surprises when I took the coach's seat. For instance, in a game with Indiana Central, they had the winning run on third base in the bottom of the ninth with no one out. I needed to load the bases to force a double play or at least a forceout at home. But I was afraid that my young pitcher would throw a wild pitch while trying to intentionally walk two batters, so I put my second baseman back by the screen behind the catcher just in case. After two pitched balls, Indiana Central coach Bill Bright came off the bench and protested. And he was right—you cannot station a fielder, with the exception of a catcher, in foul territory.

At least on one occasion, I was on the right side of the rules. Our college baseball team went to Manchester College for a doubleheader. As we approached the playing field, I glanced at first base line and thought it looked long. During first game as I was walking to the bench from the first base line, I kept looking at the distance between home and first base. I just couldn't get it out of my head. We lost the first game and hit into two double plays. In between the games, I mentioned to the home plate umpire that first base looked a little far down the line. The Manchester coach, having overheard my comment, insisted that he personally measured the bases and that they were correct. Well, he pushed my hot button.

"I want them measured," I said

"We don't have time, and the tape is in the maintenance building," he said.

I faced him and said emphatically, "We'll wait."

By now, both teams knew my demand. The tape was brought out, and the umpires measured the baseline, which was supposed to be 90 feet including the first base bag. Sure enough, the base was off.

"Your base is 90 feet and then the bag," the umpire said. "The base is one width of the bag too far."

The coach had to change all three bases, and we won the second game.

My players couldn't believe that I could spot the error in the length of the baseline. I was surprised myself. I guess because I had sat through thousands of innings, many in the dugout on the first base side, my instincts took over.

Wildcats

My first year out of pro baseball, 1960, I had a request from Dale W. McMillen, founder of Central Soya Company, an international feed company. Mr. Mac was nearly 80 years old and had shared his wealth with Fort Wayne, Indiana, giving generously to schools, parks, churches, and other causes and endeavors.

Mr. Mac told me he had just learned that some boys and girls were being denied the chance to play baseball in organized games if they didn't make a Little League team. He said, "I want to start a baseball program for all the kids who can't make Little League, and you're going to help me."

He hired coaches from the school system and set up a program called "Wildcat Baseball" in all the city parks. He made a few rules: No parents at games. All boys and girls received a cap and Wildcat shirt, provided that they could prove they had earned the money themselves. Mr. Mac encouraged good morals and a healthy lifestyle. The kids responded in big numbers, and by late August, some 5,000 had joined the Wildcats, including some children who were physically disabled.

Mr. Mac said, "OK, Carl, our year-end program is set for McMillen Park. I want you to get Jackie Robinson to come for the celebration." Jackie accepted. The next year was another big success. Mr. Mac said, "OK, Carl, I want you to get Bob Feller." Bob accepted. The third year we had another 5,000 kids. Mr.

Mac said, "Now, Carl, I want you to get Ted Williams." I said, "Mr. Mac, Ted doesn't do many appearances. He does endorse sports equipment for Sears Roebuck." Mr. Mac called the chairman of Sears. Ted came. At McMillen Park at Fort Wayne, Indiana, on a dusty dirt ball diamond, in front of 5,000 Wildcat kids, Bob Feller pitched to Ted Williams, Jackie fielded in the infield, and I shagged fly balls in the outfield. The Wildcats went wild when Williams hit towering balls over all of the bicycles in the outfield, over the trees, and over the parking lot.

Mr. Mac died a long time ago, but thanks to his foundation, the Wildcat program is still alive and well. Oh, yes, when my doctor, Charles King, retired, I chose a new young physician, Philip Goshert, as our family doctor. When he saw me, he said, "We've met before. I was a Wildcat kid at McMillen Park."

Passing the "Buck"

After I left professional baseball as a player, I had several baseball offers and even some broadcast opportunities. ABC signed me to a 13-week *Game of the Week* contract as a color analyst with Jack Buck as the regular play-by-play man. Jack was the regular broadcaster for the St. Louis Cardinals, and he was a real class act.

Most of our games were in San Francisco covering the Willie Mays-led Giants, who were picked to win the National League pennant, at brand-new Candlestick Park. After one Saturday game, Jack and I had a free evening before we caught a redeye midnight flight back to the East Coast, so he wanted to take me to a great Chinese restaurant in Chinatown called The Rickshaw. We grabbed a cab and headed for Chinatown, but the cabbie couldn't find The Rickshaw. We just kept driving around and around because Jack insisted it was in the area. Finally he told the cabbie to stop and said, "Come on, Carl. We'll find it."

Progress Day for the Wildcat Baseball League gave Jackie Robinson, me, Mr. Mac, Bob Feller, and Ted Williams a few laughs in 1962. *(Courtesy of Wildcat Baseball, Fort Wayne, Indiana)*

After a futile search, we still could not find The Rickshaw. Just then we saw a well-dressed couple coming our way. As they approached, we could tell they were Asian, probably Chinese. Jack said confidently, "Now we'll find out where it is." He went up to the couple and asked where the restaurant was. The couple paused for a second and in very halting, broken English the gentleman said, "Ah sa-ree, we're from Chi-cah-go."

Jack gave up, and we went for Italian.

Although his sense of direction outside of the press box didn't help us that night, Jack's direction behind the mike encouraged me to stay in broadcasting. I worked with him on KMOX as a guest on several random broadcasts after *Game of the Week*. He had a beautiful pace when calling a game; he was never in a hurry and he never second-guessed the manager. He was clever and witty.

In a lopsided game in Washington, the Senators were getting killed, which incidentally also kills a broadcast. It's tough to make a game interesting if there is not much of a game going on. But Jack was great at making something out of nothing. He would add a twist to the action that would make it amusing. For example, when he mentioned the Senators' catcher Hal Naragon, Jack said, ". . . of course, you know what a naragon is—that's a no-sided figure."

Fantasy Land

One of the carryover dividends from my baseball career was being an instructor at several Dodger fantasy camps. The camp is for those who love baseball and dreamed of wearing a major league uniform. In real life, they are physicians, attorneys, judges, corporate presidents, schoolteachers, and those from a wide variety of vocations. For about $4,000 they can come to Dodgertown baseball complex at Vero

Broadcasting great Jack Buck and I cover the *Game of the Week* for NBC in 1960. *(Carl Erskine Collection)*

Beach, Florida, and spend a week living with, talking with, and playing baseball with some 20 former major-leaguers.

Here they learn the techniques of pitching, hitting, fielding, bunting, and base running, just like the pros. Teams are selected, games are played, stats are kept, and nightly awards are given for the "Play of the Day" and also for the most valuable player of each team for that day.

The MVP award itself is an odd-looking plastic toy figure called Mr. Potato Head. At one time the "real" Dodger players used one of these plastic dolls to honor their best player of the day in a kind of gag award. However, it did mean something special because it paid tribute to a good day in the big leagues.

Now, you can imagine how a fantasy camper feels when his name is called and he goes up front to receive this award. As crazy as it seems, this award may be the highlight of this person's life.

One such camper came forward one night when his name was called. He was the nonathletic type, about age 55, and with eyes wide in disbelief, he accepted the trophy. Then in a voice deep with emotion, he said, "Oh, my God, this goes in my casket."

Pushed to Success

One of the toughest challenges faced by a major league baseball player is unseen. It involves the difficult adjustments that must be made when a successful sports figure moves to the real world of making a living outside the sport.

Most players of my era were signed as teenagers and had no education beyond high school and no business experience or training to use after baseball. I was 19 when I signed and 32 when I retired. I was married with four children.

The playmakers at Dodger fantasy camp receive their awards. *(Courtesy of the Dodgers)*

I was attracted to the life insurance business because it required no investment and I could work in my home area; however, selling is not for everyone, nor is a job that pays only on commission. If you're not a real self-starter, don't try commission selling.

Ironically, baseball helped me through one of my lowest days as a salesman. It was one of the few times I was ever really down. I couldn't get motivated to sell insurance. I didn't know who to see, and I was uncomfortable at being persistent. I felt lost.

On this particular morning, I was dressed but didn't want to leave the house. I looked in the mirror; my eyes were glassy, and I was whipped. About 10:00 a.m. the phone rang. It was T. Franklin Miller, one of the leading citizens of Anderson, Indiana. Dr. Miller was a minister/businessman and very well respected. He said, "Carl, I'm chairman of the United Way, and today is our kickoff luncheon. We just got a call that our speaker can't make it. Would you come and speak for us? Just give us a little motivational talk." Boy, this was the last thing I needed. However, saying no to Dr. Miller was very hard. I stammered a few comments about short notice, etc., then Dr. Miller said, "Well, Carl, you know you'll be among friends." When I said OK and hung up, I couldn't believe I had accepted.

I had only about an hour to try and put some thoughts together. I hit on the theme "Expect the Unexpected," and I talked about how we often don't set our sights high enough, especially when raising money. I used several illustrations to make my point. I closed by saying, "Today in the fourth game of the 1962 World Series, in spite of baseball being over a hundred years old, something unexpected will happen that's never happened before in a World Series. About the time I was saying this, a little second baseman for San Francisco, Chuck Hiller, hit his first and only World Series home run, a grand slam. It was the first grand slam in the history of the National League in World Series play. It beat the Yankees, too.

My speech went well, but more importantly, I learned a valuable lesson. Looking inward with self-pity is defeating, but giving of yourself where you can help others revives your spirit. During the next decade, I stayed among the top 10 in sales for our insurance company.

Old-Time Religion

Tommy Henrich was an outstanding New York Yankees outfielder and a sweet hitter.

He was also a great ambassador for the game of baseball and a sensational storyteller. He told me that the following actually happened during the 1965 World Series.

Tommy was attending the opening game of the World Series with his friend and Hall of Fame teammate Lefty Gomez. Gomez was a comic without really trying. He always seemed to find the most unique humor in any situation.

Sandy Koufax was scheduled to pitch this opening game against the Minnesota Twins, but because it fell on a Jewish holiday, which Sandy always honored, he was automatically excused for the day. Don Drysdale was moved up one day in the pitching rotation to pitch the opener. In the third inning, the Twins got to Drysdale for five runs. Walt Alston, the Dodger manager, went to the mound and made a pitching change. As Alston and Drysdale walked off the field toward the dugout, Gomez said to Henrich, "I know what Alston is saying to Drysdale."

Tommy said, "How do you know what Alston is saying?"

"Believe me," said Lefty, "I know exactly what Alston is saying."

"What's he saying?" said Tommy.

"He's saying, 'Why couldn't you have been Jewish instead of Koufax?'"

Hank Aaron

Henry Aaron's name is the first one listed alphabetically in *The Baseball Encyclopedia*. Of course, he's also first in career home runs with 755.

I once received a fascinating document prepared by an Aaron fan who wished me to sign in several appropriate places. This document was a listing of every home run Aaron hit on his way to breaking Babe Ruth's record of 714 career home runs. It listed the date, the opponent, the inning, the number of men on base, and a space for the signature of the pitcher who gave up that particular home run. The fan requested my signature on the following: home runs Nos. 20, 25, 44, 97, and 123. (These homers were hit during a five-year span.)

The document had already been signed by several other pitchers. My teammate Don Drysdale leads the list with 17. One irony on the list was that the first home run pitch was thrown by Vic Raschi, while the record-breaking 715th was thrown by Al Downing. Both were former star pitchers for the New York Yankees.

I once asked Henry Aaron in a radio interview what his theory was on hitting. He simply said, "My theory on hitting is: attack the ball before it attacks you."

Moon Rocks

In 1969 the world watched the incredible moon landing. Neil Armstrong and Buzz Aldrin actually sent back TV pictures of themselves walking, raising the American flag, hitting a golf ball, and collecting rock samples on the lunar surface.

Shortly after that landing, I attended a weekend Old-Timers' Game at Shea Stadium. On Friday the major league game was rained out. The Saturday afternoon game was also rained out, and on Sunday afternoon, it was still raining. By now, the players were stir-crazy, and so were the old-timers. Players were standing around, reading, playing cards, when finally, in frustration, somebody yelled out, "How long is it gonna rain in this damn town?" Cleon Jones, who was platooning at first base for the Mets, stood near his locker, turned around, and with his eyes wide, said, "It's gonna rain 'til they [the astronauts] put them rocks back."

In Tune

When I am asked who was the toughest hitter I ever had to face, I usually give that distinction to Stan "The Man" Musial—so named by Brooklyn fans because he hit so well in Ebbets Field. Stan was a contact hitter who hit to all fields and with good power. He was a tough out.

As the years passed, Stan and I got better acquainted at baseball functions. One of those functions took place in Louisville, shortly after A. Ray Smith, owner of the Louisville Red Birds, a Triple A team, broke a minor league attendance record by drawing more than one million paid fans. For his big celebration, he had invited a large gathering of major-leaguers.

I had dinner with Stan and his wife, Lil. Al Hirt, the famous trumpet player, provided the dinner music. After dinner, Stan pulled a harmonica out of his pocket, and I said, "What are you doing with that?" He said, "I'm going to play a tune with Al Hirt. I jokingly said, "I should have brought my harmonica." Stan pulled a second harp from his pocket and gave it to me.

Stan and I played "Oh, Them Golden Slippers" with Al Hirt. I confess it was much easier playing with Stan than playing against him.

Harry Geisel

Baseball players have a unique way of playing the game and umpiring at the same time. Pitchers are especially attuned to what each pitch is called—either a ball or a strike. When I retired from baseball, I received three or four letters from umpires saying they had enjoyed working my games. However, they added, "You didn't complain much, but, boy, did you do a lot of 'surveying' from the mound."

A former American League umpire was Harry Geisel. He spoke at numerous banquets when I was a kid in amateur baseball, and he always told a story about Yankee pitcher Lefty Gomez.

One day, Lefty was complaining about several pitches by coming off the mound and walking toward home plate. Finally, Harry warned him: "One more time, Lefty, and you're outta here!" Sure enough, a couple of pitches later, said Harry, "Here comes Lefty toward home plate. I took off my mask, ready to give him the heave-ho, when he raised his hand and said, 'No, I didn't come down here to argue about that pitch, Mr. Geisel. I just wanted to ask you how you spell your name.'" "What?" said Harry. "Your last name," said Lefty. "How do you spell it?" "Why, it's spelled G-E-I-S-E-L," said Harry. "That's just what I thought," said Lefty, "one eye."

You Stand on Where You Sit

During the 1970s, a television show was introduced called *Sports Challenge*. The game pitted three-member teams from famous lineups in various sports against each other. Three of us from the Brooklyn Dodgers made up one of the teams: Jackie Robinson, Duke Snider, and me.

Our team proved to be a winning combination, with Jackie and Duke showing poise under pressure as usual. Duke was especially sharp and would hit his buzzer quickly when Dick Enberg, the host, would ask a sports question. After several rounds of questions, with certain numbers of points scored for correct answers, came the final round. The idea here was to identify the "mystery guest" by viewing a silhouette on a screen and listening to clues given by Enberg. This last round carried the biggest point value, so a team well behind in points could catch up or win with the correct answer.

As we were preparing to film a segment before a live audience, Jackie had to leave the set and go to the property room and change his tie. While he was backstage, he accidentally ran into the mystery guest in the hallway. It was baseball Hall of Famer Frank Robinson.

The director had to announce a delay while the staff located another mystery guest. Meanwhile, we waited in the Los Angeles studio and Duke began to speculate on whom they could find quickly in the area. After he discounted a few possibilities, Duke said, "Hey! Right across the street from this studio is television station KTLA, and Tommy Harmon, the great football Hall of Famer, is the sports director over there. Let's be ready."

When the game progressed to the final round, our team was trailing the Baltimore Colts, headed by their great quarterback, Johnny Unitas. The silhouette was flashed on the screen, and before Dick Enberg could give the first clue, Duke hit his buzzer. "Tommy Harmon," he said. Dodgers win again.

In yet another encounter, the Brooklyn Dodgers were matched against three famous jockeys: Eddie Arcaro, Johnny Longden, and Willie Shoemaker.

When Enberg asked the name of the racehorse that holds the record for coming from farthest behind to win a race, Duke again was first with the buzzer. "Silky Sullivan," he answered correctly. And to think, Shoemaker was the jockey riding Silky Sullivan that day!

Back Home Again

I always appreciated the sportswriters and broadcasters who were a part of my years in baseball, and I tried to accommodate their requests for interviews. Only once did I ever refuse.

Gil Hodges and I were both from Indiana. We were both scouted by Stan Feezle of Indianapolis and played together for a decade in Brooklyn and Los Angeles. A fixture at Ebbets Field was our organist, Gladys Gooding. She not only could play well but also had a real knack for playing a song at the most appropriate time. One of my fondest memories of Ebbets Field is hearing her play "Back Home Again in Indiana" each time I would warm up to start a game or be called in from the bullpen. She'd always strike up that tune when Gil would hit a home run. Gil and I both had strong ties to our home state, and Gladys never missed a chance to play that song for us.

Following Gil's playing days, he became an outstanding manager and led the 1969 Mets to a Cinderella World Series championship. Then the shock came in the spring of 1972, when he died suddenly of a massive heart attack at age 51.

Several of us attended his funeral as honorary pallbearers at the Brooklyn Catholic Church, where he was a member. At the conclusion of the service, we followed the closed casket as it was wheeled up the aisle and outside. At that moment the organist played "Back Home Again in Indiana." That really hit me hard. As I stepped through the big open double doors of the church, Howard Cosell was waiting there with his camera crew. He held a mike in front of me and asked a question. I was so choked up, I couldn't speak. One look and even the brash Howard Cosell knew that wasn't the time for an interview.

Then and Now

There's one baseball story handed down through the years that serves as a great illustration when someone asks a player if, in fact, the old-timers were really better ballplayers than the current players. Of course, it's impossible to fairly compare different eras; however, the story goes that Duke Snider was asked how he thought a great player of the past, such as Ty Cobb, would bat against modern pitchers. Duke thought a moment, then said, "Oh, he'd probably hit around a .250 to .300 average."

"Two fifty?" came the surprised reply. "Why, Ty Cobb batted .367 lifetime over a 24-year career. You mean he'd only hit .250 today against modern pitchers?" "Well," said Duke, "you have to realize that Ty Cobb would be over 90 years old."

The Pen

Sportswriters are vital to the game of baseball. Their writing skills and their perspective on the game help to sustain the fans' interest and fix in history epic moments, relived for decades by fans, whether they were at a particular game or just read about it.

Sometimes a war of words is fought in print between a player and a writer when, over time, a disagreement escalates into a running battle. Jackie Robinson and Jim Murray of the *L.A. Times* had a strong and ongoing paper fight.

At the 1972 World Series in Cincinnati, Jackie was at the game. He was now past 50 years old, very gray, and had almost lost his eyesight because of diabetes. Jackie happened to find himself face to face with Jim Murray. Time had passed since their fierce exchange in various columns. Jackie stuck out his hand to Jim and then said, "I'm sorry, Jim, I can't see you any more." Jackie died later that October.

Jim Murray wrote a classic column about Jackie, reminding readers of Jackie's courage as a player, his highly competitive
spirit, and Jackie and Jim's last meeting at the 1972 World
Series. He closed his story by saying, "I'm sorry, Jackie, I can't
see you any more."

Boys of Summer

Roger Kahn joined the Dodgers' beat as a sportswriter for
the *New York Herald-Tribune* in 1952 and, of course,
later wrote the book *The Boys of Summer*, etching the
Brooklyn Dodgers of those years into the minds of baseball fans
everywhere. But writing a book is like a nine-inning baseball
game; the last couple of chapters, like innings, are hard to finish.
Roger had that experience.

In the early 1970s, several of the Dodgers were invited to
attend a big B'nai B'rith dinner in New York City. After the
banquet, Roger grabbed me and said we had to talk. We went
to Toots Shor's restaurant, and Roger started drinking scotch
and pouring his heart out. "I can't finish this book. I'm broke
and I'm dry. I keep wondering who's going to read this stuff."
He was low. Now I'm no psychologist, and I was having a hard
time knowing how to respond. I said all of the standard stuff
like "You can't disappoint this team. They're counting on you
to write this book." Roger just had another scotch and continued his down mood. I tried to be a good listener, but I didn't
have any real answers.

Finally, a thought hit me. Dick Young of the *Daily News*
had been a beat writer with us much longer than Roger. Dick
had a strong identity with the Dodgers. I said to Roger, "How
would you like to wake up tomorrow morning and find out that
Dick Young had written your book?" That comment sobered
him up a bit.

I helped Roger to a cab, gave the driver his address, and we parted. He did finish *The Boys of Summer*. I later sent Roger a poem by Robert Service entitled "My Masterpiece." The last stanza of the poem reads:

A humdrum way I go tonight
For all I hoped and dreamed remote
Too late . . . a better man must write
That little book I never wrote.

Roger framed the poem and placed it by his fireplace in his home at Croton on the Hudson, New York.

The once ill-fated book went on to be a significant piece of baseball literature and a financial success, so much so that *Sports Illustrated* magazine selected *The Boys of Summer* as the greatest baseball book ever written in 2002.

Out of Sight

After *The Boys of Summer* was released in 1972, the publisher held a book signing at the famous Tavern on the Green in Central Park. The Boys of Summer—Duke Snider, Pee Wee Reese, Jackie Robinson, George Shuba, Carl Furillo, and Clem Labine—were there. It was a good reunion for this Dodger team because we hadn't seen each other often after our careers ended.

I stood off to one side and talked with Jackie. He was a little heavy and showing lots of gray. I asked him if he was playing golf. Jackie could beat almost anyone at golf, pin-pong, tennis, poker, bridge—you name it. He said, "No, I can't see the ball." I chuckled, thinking he was referring to his paunch in front.

Then a lady came over and asked us to sign a copy of the book. When she handed the book to Jackie, he turned to me and said, "Carl, start my hand on the page. I'm afraid I'll run

JACKIE ROBINSON CONSTRUCTION CORP.

560 SYLVAN AVENUE • ENGLEWOOD, CLIFFS, N.J. 07632
TELEPHONE: 201-871-4216

May 15, 1972

Mr. Carl Erskine
Vice President
First National Bank
Anderson, Indiana

Dear Carl:

So many people have told me of the things you
and others said on the Dick Cavitt Show. I
am sure you know how appreciative I am, but
it could never have happened apart from the
cooperative spirit of teamwork and selfless
unity. It certainly must give you a warm
feeling, just as it does me, to know the
role each played in Mr. Rickey's successful
venture. Our efforts did make this land a
little better; and while we have gone our
separate ways, Roger's book brings back some
vivid memories. Frankly, I am proud. In today's world, we can look in retrospect and
say that because we were "The Boys of Summer"
much has been accomplished, culminating in a
cause for less tension.

My sincere thanks, again. It's good to know
we still remember those days.

Most sincerely,

Jackie Robinson

(Carl Erskine Collection)

off the edge." That was the first time I realized that diabetes had taken the eyesight of this gifted man.

Until then I had never understood the line in the poem by English poet Dylan Thomas that Roger Kahn had used for the title *The Boys of Summer*. The line reads, "I see the boys of summer in their ruin." Now I understood.

The Signature

One of the spinoffs from a sports career is the card show. The collecting of sports cards and sports memorabilia has produced a whole new segment of commerce. Old uniform tops, signed baseballs, caps, sports programs, etc., all take on real value in time.

Honus Wagner, a Hall of Famer and an old-time Pirate shortstop, holds the distinction of being the former player whose baseball card commanded the highest price ever paid for one—something over $1 million. Mickey Mantle's 1952 card is in the $50,000 range.

At card shows, former players are paid a contractual fee to sign autographs for three hours. Fans line up for long waits and buy a ticket for each autograph. Some players' handwriting is a bit more legible than others.

I was always taught to be proud of my name and to treat it with respect. A fan once remarked to me how clear my signature was. I told her that my teachers encouraged that. She just beamed and said, "I'm a teacher."

Walter O.

History has already recorded Walter O'Malley as the hard-nosed business tycoon who moved the Dodgers out of Brooklyn. Peter Golenbock, in his book *Bums:*

An Oral History of the Brooklyn Dodgers, quotes a Brooklyn Dodger fan as saying that the three most hated men in the world are Hitler, Mussolini, and O'Malley.

It's too late to convince any Brooklyn fan to see Walter O. differently. However, he did want to keep the Dodgers in Brooklyn. Unfortunately, a number of New York's political power brokers helped prevent the Dodgers from staying put. If O'Malley had had his way, the first domed stadium would have been built in Brooklyn.

Two incidents demonstrate a sensitive and caring side of O'Malley. As a young man, the love of his life was a college girl named Kay. Although Kay had cancer of the larynx and lost her voice, Walter was not deterred. They married, reared a large family, and she was his strong, silent partner for life. That kind of commitment deserves to be honored.

The second incident involved O'Malley inviting Betty and me and Jimmy, our son who has Down syndrome, to Dodger Stadium in 1978 to commemorate the 20th anniversary of the first game played in Los Angeles. I had pitched and won that game, so I participated in the festivities.

After an on-field ceremony, we were seated in O'Malley's luxury box, along with many dignitaries. Mr. O'Malley was being the gracious host and checking to see if anybody wanted anything to eat or drink. Most of those he asked declined because it was nearly time for the game to begin. When O'Malley got to us, he asked what we would like. Jimmy spoke up and said, "Hot dog." "What did he say?" asked Mr. O. "Two of 'em," said Jimmy. While the world watched the opening pitch, Mr. O was back in his small kitchen, fixing two hot dogs for Jimmy. I could hear Jimmy saying, "Catsup, mustard." O'Malley didn't miss a swipe with the mustard, although, for Jimmy's sake, he did miss the opening pitch of that historic game.

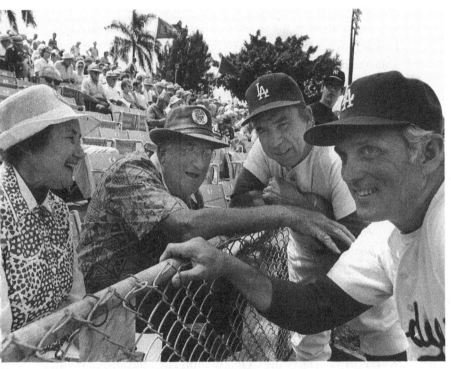

Kay and Walter O'Malley with Pee Wee Reese and me at Dodgertown's Holman Stadium. *(Courtesy of the Dodgers)*

Tracey

The Yankees and Dodgers were playing the 1978 World Series. I attended the first two games at Dodger Stadium. Before Game 1, I was in the Yankee dressing room, talking with my old teammate, Clyde King, who was working for the Yankees.

It occurred to me to tell Clyde about a 12-year-old Little League catcher named Tracey Gustin, a Yankee fan from my hometown of Anderson, Indiana, who had terminal bone cancer. Reggie Jackson, who was on the trainer's table, heard me when I asked Clyde if he thought one of the Yankees might call Tracey sometime. Reggie said, "Get the number, Clyde, I'll do it." I gave Clyde the number and then actually forgot about the incident.

The Dodgers won the first two games of the Series. I returned to Indiana and the teams went to New York. Game 3 was set for Sunday.

About one o'clock I got a call from Tracey's mother. She was so excited that she could hardly talk. "Guess what happened? The Yankees called Tracey from Yankee Stadium just now—Bob Lemon, the manager, Catfish Hunter, Reggie Jackson, Goose Gossage, Yogi Berra, and Clyde King all talked to Tracey. I even taped part of it. Tracey is on cloud nine."

The Yankees went on to win four straight and capture the World Series. Tracey died a few months later, but what a boost my old enemies gave that little boy and his family. They still play that tape.

The Prize

Competition has been an ongoing part of my life. I learned how intense it can be in sports and experienced it later in business. In fact in business it might be tougher and harder to address. At least in baseball I could easily identify my opponents—they wore a different uniform.

After living and working and playing with and against talented athletes, I found another level just as intense, just as competitive, and just as rewarding. In the Special Olympics the athletes are just that—special—because they are not gifted with exceptionally fine muscle tone, coordination, or athletic skill, but despite their handicaps, they come off the bench and into action. They come onto the field and into the game—track and field, swimming, bowling, softball, basketball, weightlifting, gymnastics, and winter sports.

The Special Olympics were started in the late 1960s by Eunice Kennedy Shriver and the Kennedy Foundation, and our son Jimmy has been a participant since 1970 when the first games were held at Indiana State University. The games are now worldwide.

There are just as many heroic stories about Special Olympians as there are about athletes in the Olympics. Plus, there is no way to measure the boost in self-esteem when Special Olympians hear their names called to the award stand and have the medals placed around their necks.

I always believe that no award could outrank receiving a World Series ring. When we received the 1955 World Series ring, I remember well the moment and the looks on the faces of my teammates, all of them great athletes—Jackie Robinson, Duke Snider, Pee Wee Reese and the rest of the lineup. This ring was a long time coming—almost 75 years. What a prize! I thought nothing could top that.

Well, you be the judge. I sat in the bleachers at Indiana State University's Olympic-size swimming pool at the ISU Special Olympic games. On the edge of the pool were six athletes waiting for the starter gun for the 50-meter freestyle event. Jimmy was in the No. 2 lane. The gun went off—there were six splashes, and they were off. Jimmy opened up a six-length lead, and I cheered like crazy. Then Jimmy noticed that some of his buddies were behind him, so he decided to wait for them to catch up.

"Go, go, Jimmy!" I screamed as I stood up.

Betty told me to sit down; I was the only one yelling and standing.

Jimmy touched the end of the pool and started back for the final 25 meters. At the end of the race, they helped him out of the water, placed him on the podium, and hung a Special Olympics gold medal around his neck.

If getting the most out of what you have is the best measurement, then Jimmy's gold medal must rank higher than a World Series ring. Certainly a team with our talents and skills was supposed to win a ring, but it was never conceived that an individual like Jimmy could compete in athletic events. Yet he did, and he won.

The ring or the medal?

You be the judge.

Throneberry

At an Old-Timers' Game at Shea Stadium one year, the theme was New York National League players from the past. Many Dodgers, Giants, and early Mets players were there.

It was also a celebration for the original Mets manager, Casey Stengel, on his 80th birthday. Casey owned many championships with the Yankees, but his early Mets teams were famous for how many different ways they could lose. After all, they were an expansion team made up of a variety of castoffs and over-the-hill players. Casey once remarked, while playing against the powerful Cincinnati "Big Red Machine" and on the way to another loss, "Look. Look at their bench—solid mahogany. Now, look at ours—driftwood."

As we were introduced to the crowd one at a time, we took our place along the foul lines extending from home plate. Casey was introduced last, and a huge birthday cake was rolled out to Casey right at home plate. Marv Throneberry, an original Met who was not known for having many skills with his first baseman's glove, said, "Hey, Casey, I had a birthday this week— nobody gave me a birthday cake." Casey said, "Well, we were gonna give you a cake, Marv, but I was afraid you'd drop it."

The Payoff

I always had a sense of gratitude for my good fortune in being a major-leaguer. Consequently, I almost never refused to accept an invitation to schools, Little League benefits, American Legion banquets, and other community events. Sometimes I tried to be in two places at once to cover all requests. Often I would leave my own kids, which was hard for Betty to understand and equally hard for me to explain, to attend some of these functions. I did come up with an Erskine saying: "When you're cheap and available, you get a lot of work."

On one occasion, I was returning home late from a function in Franklin, Indiana. I was in a hurry to get back home— too much of a hurry, because I was stopped by an Indiana state trooper. This young man could have been a poster boy for state troopers. He looked great in uniform, with everything "spit and polished." Even though I was irritated at being stopped, I had to admire the young man.

He asked me to step back to his patrol car and sit in the passenger's seat. I answered his questions and provided my license and registration. I just sat there silently as he filled out the ticket. About halfway through he stopped, starred straight ahead, said to no one in particular, "I can't give this ticket. No, I can't give this ticket."

"Is there something wrong?" I asked.

"I can't give you this ticket," he said. "When I was ten years old, you came to my Little League banquet and gave me a trophy and an autographed baseball."

Yogi

The unusual quotes from Yogi Berra seem to be endless and always amusing. It makes you wonder where he gets his inspiration.

One of his classics is "Good pitching will stop good hitting every time—and vice versa." Another is "When you come to the fork in the road, take it." Actually, that latter comment makes sense when you understand that Yogi's walk forks around a flower bed and then comes back together on the other side. It doesn't matter which side you take.

"What time is it, Yogi?" "Now," he answers.

Looking out at a spotty crowd before a game one day, some players expressed disappointment. Yogi said, "If these people don't want to come to the game, who's gonna stop 'em?" Is it in the blood, or what?

I read an interview with Yogi's son Dale. The interviewer was discussing how great it must have been for Dale to follow in his dad's footsteps by making the big leagues and wearing the pinstripes of the Yankees. He said, "Dale, you and your dad must have a lot in common." Dale answered, "Actually, our similarities are different." Now, that's got to be in the genes.

The Rifle from Reading

In 1989 I got off the plane in Philadelphia and met Peter O'Malley and Sandy Koufax in the terminal. We took a taxi to the funeral home in Reading, Pennsylvania, where Carl

Furillo was to receive his last rites. Carl had died in his sleep at age 66.

When we arrived, Johnny Podres and Billy Loes were already there. Fern Furillo and her sons met us near the door and thanked us for coming. Then she turned to Peter and asked, "Would you say a few words during the service?" "Well, I would, but I think it would be more appropriate for a teammate to do that," he said softly and put a hand on my shoulder. "Carl, you're the right one for that." I looked at him. The service was about to start in a few minutes. I swallowed hard. "Okay," I said.

Now I didn't have time to get nervous as I tried to put my thoughts in some semblance of order. A few minutes into the service, I was asked to step up to the mike. I had no notes, only the genuine memories of a man who was my teammate for 12 years and for whom I had a great respect. I talked about how consistent he had been in right field and at bat and how diligently he approached his job. Then I described something I had seen him do from his position in right field—he had thrown runners out at all bases, even first base. I recalled how I had seen him in two fights, neither of which he started but both of which he won. Everyone knew that Carl was physically strong and a no-nonsense ballplayer, had an exceptional right arm, and was outspoken in his intolerance of "half-hearted" efforts by players, but I think what I said next surprised them: Carl was a sensitive person. I often fished or attended events with Carl. He was always surrounded by his Italian friends, and he seemed to need that. There were many of us on the team who lived in the Bay Ridge section of Brooklyn and we would carpool to and from the games. I know Carl felt left out sometimes and that bothered him, but he was good with kids and faithful to his family. His gruff exterior often obscured his more tender side. It was like our former manager Charlie Dressen would say, "It's like comparing dirt to ice cream"; well, Carl was like steel and velvet.

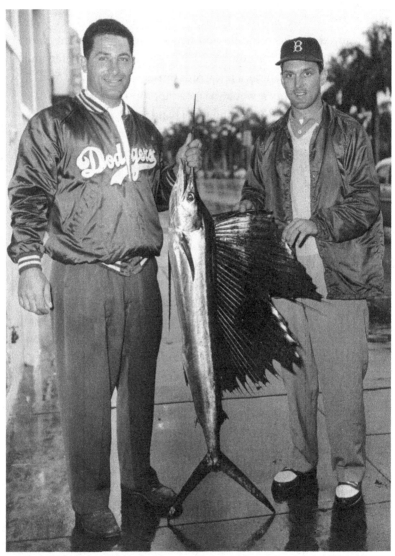

Carl Furillo and I display our success on one of many fishing trips in Florida. *(Carl Erskine Collection)*

Four Greatest

Roy Campanella said that to play baseball, "You had to have a lot of little boy in you." Well, I never felt more like a kid than the day in Shea Stadium when I was standing with about 50 others, former major league players, all in uniforms along the foul lines. We had been individually introduced. Then the announcer said, "Please direct your attention to the center field gate. In a moment it will open, and through it will walk four of the greatest center fielders in the history of baseball."

Walking in from the gate, four abreast, were Duke Snider, Joe DiMaggio, Willie Mays, and Mickey Mantle. Although I had roomed with Duke for 11 big-league seasons, the little boy in me wanted to run out to these four greats and get their autographs.

Greener Grass

I'm sometimes asked why I chose baseball as a profession. My honest answer is that actually baseball chose me. I was blessed with some special talents in baseball. The scouts sought me out, and eventually I was signed with the Dodgers. However, one of my strong interests since high school has been the poetic things in life. Reading talented poets such as Robert Service and Robert Frost made me want to write poetry too. So over the years I have penned several and kept them in a personal file.

Roger Kahn was a close friend of Robert Frost. Secretly Frost dreamed of becoming a baseball pitcher: "Nothing flatters me more than to have it assumed that I could write prose, unless it be to have it assumed that I once pitched a baseball with distinction."

Duke Snider, Joe DiMaggio, Willie Mays, and Mickey Mantle get together for an Old-Timers' Game at Shea Stadium. *(Carl Erskine Collection)*

In a frivolous mood Frost wrote this ditty:

Never ask of money spent
Where the spender thinks it went
Nobody was ever meant
To remember or invent
What he did with every cent.

My own parody after having had to answer sportswriters' questions about a bad pitch or being saved by a great catch:

Never ask a pitcher's thought
If the pitch went where it ought
And found the corner which it sought
Behaving just as it was taught
Dispel the vicious drive was caught.

I Blew It

One of the hobbies I kept up during my playing days was playing the harmonica. I usually carried one with me on the road and played only when my roomie, Duke Snider, was out. As the years passed, I continued, but never in public. Then some of my buddies who had a country band encouraged me to play with them. This eventually led to me having my own group.

My biggest personal gig came when Peter O'Malley of the Dodgers asked me to play the national anthem at Dodger Stadium. In fact, because Montreal was in town, I was to do both "Oh, Canada" and "The Star-Spangled Banner." So, in front of 45,000 fans and facing three video cameras for big-screen "Diamond Vision," I made it through both anthems. It was like pitching both ends of a doubleheader.

I show my form on the harmonica in Dodger Stadium "Diamond Vision." *(Courtesy of the Dodgers)*

You Could Look It Up

I'm often asked, as most major-leaguers are, to visit schools and talk to kids about good values and a healthy lifestyle. There are numerous ways to use baseball illustrations to show how teamwork, unselfishness, obeying the rules, and keeping your bodies in shape can produce a winning lifestyle.

A program called Character Counts is a valuable concept in building good character. The concept uses six pillars of good character—Trustworthiness, Respect, Responsibility, Fairness, Caring, and Citizenship. I have often used six pitches that a pitcher can throw to show how making the right choice in different circumstances produces success. I write the six pillars around the stitches on a new baseball and tell the class that good character holds your life together just like the stitches hold the baseball together. Then I sign the ball, put it in a holder, and leave it at the school as a reminder.

Usually after my presentation there is some time for questions. Every time someone always asks, "How many home runs did you hit?" Instead of confessing to my lone round-tripper, I tell them that I roomed with Hall of Famer Duke Snider, and together we hit 408.

Roy Campanella

One of the most remarkable players and personalities in Dodger history is Roy Campanella. Roy was my catcher from 1948 until his injury in an auto accident in January 1958. The accident left Roy paralyzed from the neck down with only minimal use of his arms, but not his hands. He lived in a wheelchair for over 30 years. He died in 1993.

In spite of his physical handicap, Roy had an immeasurable amount of determination, patience, and loving spirit. Roy was a

man of faith and once told me the chair wouldn't whip him—
that it was between him and the Good Lord. Roy never lost his
dignity, nor did he lose his gratitude for life.

Roy was an experienced catcher because of his years in the
Negro Leagues, as well as winter baseball in Central America,
South America, and Mexico. Consequently, our young pitch-
ing staff depended on him in calling pitches during the game.
Roy would say, "Now you young pitchers just throw what ol'
Roy calls and I'll make you a winner." I lockered next to Roy,
so when I would lose a game, I would bring in the newspaper
box score and show it to Roy. I would show him that it said,
"Erskine, losing pitcher." Then I would ask him if it shouldn't
say, "Campanella, losing catcher." He would chuckle and say,
"You can always shake me off."

I once took a business associate, Bob Wright, to visit Roy
in a New York hospital. Periodically, Roy would have to be
readmitted for treatment of large bedsores caused by his inabil-
ity to feel or move while seated in his wheelchair. He was face-
down in his bed.

After an hour's visit with Roy, we said goodbye. Outside,
Bob said, "I thought we went there to cheer him up. He made
me feel terrific." Roy never felt sorry for himself; he always had
a sweet spirit and talked about what he had, not what he had
lost. Also, he showed great interest in others and their problems.
He was an encourager.

At a Dodger reunion many years after our playing days, I
was in the clubhouse, talking with teammates. Roy was there in
his motorized wheelchair, chatting with his buddies. He spotted
me and called me over. Funny thing, whenever I saw Roy, I
never saw the chair, only his sharp dress—shined shoes and this
warm, wonderful man. "How you doin', Ersk?" (Remember, I
had pitched over 300 games to Roy and also five World Series.)
Roy knew I had recent hip surgery from an old baseball injury.
He also knew about Jimmy, our son with Down syndrome. I
said I was doing fine. Then he said, "How's Jimmy doing?" I

What better place for former teammates to get together than Cooperstown, New York? On hand for Don Drysdale's induction into the Hall of Fame in 1984 are (left to right) me, Duke Snider, Pee Wee Reese, Sandy Koufax, and Drysdale. In front is Roy Campanella. *(Courtesy of the Dodgers)*

told him about Jimmy's swimming and bowling in the Special Olympics and his work at a sheltered workshop. Roy said, "I think about you and Betty a lot, and I say a prayer for you almost daily."

You can see that Roy was right. He did make the right calls, and defeat was not in him.

Earnshaw

Baseball and American history are so intertwined that the Smithsonian Institution once asked me to lend a hand. One day I received a call from the Smithsonian's curator, who told me that a baseball display was being prepared and that there was one specific item I might be able to provide.

Pitchers almost all drag their toe after pushing off the pitching rubber when delivering a pitch. Shoes of the past were made of very light kangaroo hide; consequently, for a right-handed pitcher, the right inside toe of the shoe would wear out quickly.

An older pitcher named George Earnshaw, who pitched in the American League from 1928 to 1936, had designed a toe plate. He took his shoe to a cobbler and instructed him to sew a heavy piece of rawhide leather on the toe to absorb the punishment caused by the constant dragging. This plate was also used by other pitchers. When I learned of the toe plate in 1948, I began to have my shoes fixed the same way.

The Smithsonian asked me for a pair of my shoes with the Earnshaw toe plate to display.

From our great Dodger teams of my era, there are seven who are members of the Hall of Fame at Cooperstown. Although I have not been elected to a spot in the hall, to my knowledge, I'm the only one invited to be in the Smithsonian.

Buck

One of the most delightful characters to play in the old Negro Leagues was Buck O'Neil. Buck was just a little early in his career to benefit from Jackie Robinson's breaking the color barrier.

This man has a sweet spirit and both a loving and forgiving heart. At a banquet in San Diego in 1997, Buck was there to honor the 50th anniversary of Jackie's entry into the major leagues. He delighted the crowd with his comments. Among them were the following:

"Oh, I don't have any hate in my heart. Sure, I missed the big leagues, but I got no hate in me. Well, yes, I do. I hate cancer. It took my wonderful wife. And I hate drugs that got hold of my nephew. But I'm thankful for my baseball days and thankful for my ability to play the game."

At his advanced age, there was something else Buck was grateful for. "You know," Buck said, "I'm 86 years old, and I got all of my organs. Some of them still work."

Longevity Pays Off

Don Zimmer signed into pro baseball as a teenager. Zimmer, an adviser for the Tampa Bay Devil Rays, has never gotten out of a baseball uniform in 55 years. He was once heir apparent to Pee Wee Reese as shortstop for the Dodgers but was severely beaned twice, and that shortened his playing career. He did spend 12 seasons with the Dodgers, Cubs, Reds, and Washington Senators after playing three years in the minors.

In his 15 seasons as a player, Zimmer's total income—including his World Series shares in 1955, 1956, and 1959—was less than his one check in 1998 when the Yankees won a record 125 games, including postseason play. His 1998 World Series check for a full share was $318,000.

When Zimmer was asked what his job was as a bench coach, he said, "I sit next to the manager. When he puts on the hit-and-run or steal sign and it works, I say, 'Nice call, Skipper.' When it doesn't work, I get up and go to the water cooler."

My Idol

One of my rewards for being a former major league player is serving on the Board of Directors of the Baseball Assistance Team (BAT). This foundation, set up by baseball commissioner Peter Ueberroth in 1986, is designed to assist any former major league player and his family, as well as umpires, front office scouts, former Negro League players, and any other member of the baseball family who demonstrates true need. During the first 12 years of BAT, a total of some $6 million was granted to qualified recipients, all of it provided in strict confidence.

The money that supports BAT comes from various sources, but the main fundraiser is an annual dinner in New York, where 1,500-plus pay an average of $500 per plate to attend. A major league player is at every table. Preceding the dinner is a lavish reception at which dinner guests are able to rub elbows and get autographs from the major-leaguers, some of whom are Hall of Famers. It is a great honor to be invited to attend this function.

At a recent reception, I was approached by an enthusiastic fan who said, "I can't believe I'm actually standing next to you and talking with you, my childhood idol." After a few minutes, he left, only to return in 10 minutes and repeat the performance. Naturally, I thanked him and wished him well. As the dinner call came, the crowd began exiting the reception and heading toward the ballroom. Again, this same fan approached me. Again, he stated how much in awe he was to be in my presence. Finally, he said, "This is the night of my life. Believe me, I'll never forget you, Clem, I'll never forget you." I guess Clem Labine, our great relief pitcher, relieved me so often that we must look alike.

Baseball Ain't Cricket

In 1997 I was invited back to Dodger Stadium to celebrate the 40th anniversary of the first game played in Los Angeles, a game that I had pitched in 1958.

After the on-field festivities were complete, I went to the Dodgers' private box. Peter O'Malley and his family had been the last family to own a major league team; Peter had sold the Dodgers to Fox Network and its owner Rupert Murdoch earlier in the year. Murdoch, at age 73, was watching his team for the first time.

Around the third inning, one of Murdoch's top executives told me that Murdoch would like to speak with me. I was introduced, we shook hands, and I took the seat next to him. Murdoch, who had paid $311 million for the Dodgers, asked, "Can you tell me what it means when they say, 'The men are in scoring position'?"

Well, I thought he was just kidding with me, so I just smiled back at him. I was sure he was joking.

He must have sensed my disbelief, because he quickly said, "I am from Australia, and I know cricket, not baseball."

So I explained to him that normally runners on second or third base were considered in scoring position. He then asked me to explain the squeeze play, which I did.

But in the back of my mind, I was thinking, "I wonder why someone hadn't sold this man the Brooklyn Bridge."

Perfect 10

The following quartet of pitchers belongs to a special brotherhood in which hitters are not allowed. Together they pitched 90 innings of no-hit, no-run baseball.

Bob Feller had three no-hit, no-run games (he also had 12 one-hitters); Sandy Koufax had four (one was a perfect game); Bob Gibson had one; and I had two. That makes 10 in all.

One distinction I can claim that the other three cannot—I'm not in the Hall of Fame.

The Sacrifice

There are numerous illustrations from baseball that reflect real life. For instance, a sacrifice bunt illustrates how an individual player gives up his opportunity for a hit so that he can advance a base runner for the good of the whole team.

Many baseball careers were interrupted by World War II, the Korean War, and the Vietnam War. In World War II alone, 5,400 professional baseball players served in the armed forces. More than 50 were killed in action; many others were injured, which either shortened or ended their careers. That's a real-life sacrifice.

Veterans Stadium in Philadelphia was so named to honor U.S. military veterans dating back to the American Revolution.

I once visited Pointe-du-Hoc on the Normandy Coast of France. High cliffs there overlook the Utah and Omaha beaches. I stood at the spot where, on June 6, 1944, D-Day, 225 specially trained U.S. Army Rangers scaled these cliffs against seemingly impossible odds to hold a position until reinforcements arrived. Only 90 survived. In all, several thousand Americans lost their lives that day and in the harrowing days

Perfect 10 hurlers (left to right): Bob Feller, Sandy Koufax, Bob Gibson, and me. *(Carl Erskine Collection)*

that followed. Rows and rows of white crosses mark their graves. Of course, Europe was subsequently liberated, and the war was eventually won.

What a price! What a sacrifice! I had kept a diary of our trip, writing a humorous limerick each day. This day, however, I was inspired to write the following:

The Sacrifice
Can we total the debt that we owe
To so many whom we'll never know?
Each life sacrificed
In a way was like Christ
We are free because they took the blow.

A Long Look

It's fun to look back at days and events that have long since passed. Viewing one's life in hindsight helps a person understand more clearly what was truly important or significant at a particular moment. Well, aside from the personal thrills, two extremely significant and historic events were born and are still alive.

The Jackie Robinson era—highlighted by his courageous contribution to baseball and America at large—showed the world that the dignity of the individual is paramount in a free society. Jackie was a thrilling player to watch. He was an intense competitor. He was high-spirited.

Why did Branch Rickey pick Jackie over so many other great black players? To me there were several reasons. Jackie was raised to have spiritual discipline and respect the dignity of every individual. He was intelligent, educated, refined, and cultured. He was married to a beautiful girl named Rachel. She matched Jackie in all of the above categories. Mr. Rickey knew he had a man who could play, could understand the challenge, and had

Jimmy Erskine at Dodgertown. *(Carl Erskine Collection)*

stability on and off the field. Jackie opened hearts and minds. He brought a new sensitivity to our society.

In 1960, Betty and I had our fourth child, Jimmy—born with Down syndrome. His world was a lot like Jackie's had been back in 1946. Through misinformation and lack of understanding, there was little opportunity for Jimmy and others like him. But Betty and I have watched a second significant social change and acceptance. Jimmy has benefited from special education, the Special Olympics, and an array of services that weren't available until after 1960. More importantly, society now looks at Jimmy and other Down syndrome people with respect, admiration, and a newfound acceptance.

Jimmy accompanies Betty and me to Dodgertown, the same baseball complex where I trained for 12 seasons. Former manager Tommy Lasorda and the other Dodgers are his buddies. Tommy has outfitted Jimmy with a full Dodger uniform. Jimmy takes his place right on the bench at fantasy camps. He loves the game—and those who play the game love him.

Jackie and Jimmy, two of my best buddies, changed the face of America.

(Photo by Ozzie Sweet)

What's The Difference?

I was 21 when I first met Jackie Robinson and became his teammate for nine seasons with the Brooklyn Dodgers. As I write this story, I have now been 21 four-plus times, thus allowing me a clear long-range perspective on the magnitude of what Jackie accomplished and what he didn't accomplish. All of the obvious things are there—his greatness as a player, his one-man-against-the-world role as he faced segregation alone. The role Branch Rickey as his mentor played and the off-field support of his wife Rachel are also part of his story. The movie *42* captures for history's sake the bitterness that Jackie had to suppress because of his commitment to turn the other cheek. I watched as he took his frustration out on the baseball. He hit it, he caught it, he threw it, and he outran it all alone on the biggest, brightest, most critical stage of New York major league baseball. This was affirmative action in the raw. No one could help him. Not his mother Mallie, Rachel, Mr. Rickey, or even his teammates. He alone had to prove that he belonged . . . and without question he did.

Jackie took the knockdown pitches, the hard, steel spikes directed at him in the form of the profane, vulgar, and unceasing barrage of flack coming out of the opponent's dugout and fans on the road. Bound by the three-year gag order placed on him by Branch Rickey, I saw a demonstration of self-control not equaled anywhere else in my lifetime. There is absolutely no record written or otherwise where Jackie ever made the slightest move or look of retaliation. Not on the field, in the clubhouse, in the parking lot, on the street, in a restaurant, or anywhere. It never happened.

While Jackie was facing this and all the other indignities of not being permitted to stay in the hotel with the team, not permitted to eat in restaurants, having to just be a black man in America when he was out of uniform, he was helping the

Dodgers become a dominant team in the National League. In Jackie's ten years with the Dodgers, the team won the league championship in 1947, 1949, 1952, 1953, 1955, and 1956, plus a World Series championship in 1955, the first and only world championship in Brooklyn Dodger history.

The question is, did any of that make a difference? Although Jackie died in 1972 at age 52 from complications of diabetes, he built up a momentum in social change that proceeded by ten years the civil rights efforts of the Rev. Martin Luther King Jr. That momentum is still alive and still impacting our culture. Only Rachel and Jackie's children Sharon and David have lived to see what Jackie missed. Today black athletes dominate many major sports; there are mayors of major cities, governors, Congressmen and women of color, and yes, the President of the United States.

It is also a sad fact that black leadership has been virtually void of open support for Jackie and his efforts. In the beginning it seemed black leaders were fearful he couldn't succeed. It was too long a shot to face down two hundred years of black/white separations. But when I once told Jackie that everyone with white skin is not your enemy; he made a very insightful response. "Carl", he said, "Bigots come in all colors."

One of the black leaders of Jackie's era was the Rev. Jesse Jackson. I was present when Rev. Jackson preached at Jackie's funeral at the Riverside Baptist Church in New York City. Rev. Jackson echoed many of Jackie's admonitions to youth as he had done in the several appearances I made with Jackie in schools and youth setting—"Get prepared, be self-motivated, strive to compete, and make your career." These were virtues Jackie had hoped would be carried on and I believed he felt the powerful and persuasive voice of Jesse Jackson would do that. It did not happen. Today black leadership only recognizes Jackie as a great athlete and the first to play in the majors. But when discussing civil rights they start with Dr. King. Despite the lack of credit that Jackie has received for his participation in the civil rights movement, Jackie's momentum has been a key to social change and civil rights both then and now.

People with special needs, I believe, have benefitted from the same momentum. This population, once out of the mainstream, now enjoy a range of services such as preschool training, special education, sheltered workshops, group homes, and job placement. When a special athlete in Special Olympics wins a gold medal, I think Jackie had something to do with that. The acceptance and inclusion of those who are different has enriched our society.

When Jackie was inducted into baseball's Hall of Fame in 1962, his plaque was placed on the circular wall along with the greatest baseball players in the history of the game. He has rightfully taken his place in baseball and American history. There is something very symbolic about those plaques; they are all the same color . . . bronze.

Many Happy Returns

In 1958 one of the most important and improbable events in baseball history took place. Two National League franchises rooted for years in New York City moved to the west coast—the Brooklyn Dodgers to Los Angeles and the New York Giants to San Francisco.

Walter O'Malley, Dodger owner, is blamed by Dodger fans for moving their beloved Dodgers and also for influencing Horace Stoneham, owner of the Giants, to move. In actuality, the blame goes to the jet plane. Prior to 1958, travel in baseball had been by train and bus. That is the reason that for over a hundred years, St. Louis was the farthest major league team west.

Opening Day in Los Angeles on April 18, 1958 was a major event. Big-league baseball had finally come to the West

Coast. The season would open against the San Francisco Giants in the Los Angeles Coliseum. It would be three years before Dodger Stadium would be built. Almost eighty thousand would be in attendance.

Walt Alston, Dodger manager, gave me the honor of being the starting pitcher in this historic game. My catcher for ten seasons had been Hall of Famer Roy Campanella, but a serious auto accident in January had hospitalized Campy with paralysis from the neck down. The starting catcher in his place was rookie John Roseboro.

In the first inning of this first game in L.A., I wanted the first pitch to be a strike and it was a fastball taken by leadoff hitter Jim Davenport. When Roseboro returned the ball to me, it had so much zip on it that I caught it just a couple of inches from my face. The next two or three return pitches were the same way. John was so pumped up that he didn't realize how hard he was returning the ball and each time nearly combed me off the mound.

I called a timeout and motioned for John to meet me halfway between home plate and the mound. As he approached me I could see his eyes through his mask and they were as big as silver dollars. "What's the matter?" he asked. "Can't you see the signs?" "John," I said. "The catcher is not supposed to throw harder than the pitcher." John got the message, and we went on to win that first game in Los Angeles, 6-5.

Take a Peek

In my twelve seasons in the National League, I faced each of the other seven teams (only eight teams in each league) in some 200 innings each and had a winning edge on each team except the Giants. Against the Giants, I tallied sixteen wins and sixteen losses. Their superstar player was center fielder

Willie Mays, whom I feel was the best all-around player I ever saw.

On several occasions at various baseball functions after our playing days, Willie would corner me and say, "Yeah Carl, we called all your pitches. We knew what was coming." I always thought Willie meant the Giants had found something in my delivery that gave away my pitches. What he was actually referring to was revealed fifty years after the 1951 season. The Giants had a sign-stealing system using a powerful telescope from the center field clubhouse window, where a wire running to the Giants bullpen in right center field in the Polo Grounds hooked to a buzzer signaling "fast ball or curve." A player seated on the bullpen bench holding a white towel could then relay the pitch to the batter at home plate. The towel remaining on the player's lap: "fast ball"; the towel raised as if wiping his face: "curve ball." Josh Prager, writer for the *Wall Street Journal*, in a classic job of investigative reporting was able to get former backup catcher Sal Yvars to admit this sign-stealing arrangement, supported by other Giant players who were there and benefitted by knowing the pitches.

This enabled the Giants to come from a thirteen-and-a-half-game deficit in August of 1951 to tie the Dodgers on the final day of the season. In the playoff to decide the National League pennant, with the Dodgers leading four to two in the bottom of the ninth and two Giants on base, manager Charlie Dressen called the bullpen and brought in Ralph Branca to relieve starter Don Newcombe. On Branca's second pitch, Bobby Thomson hit the "shot heard 'round the world," a three-run walk-off home run in the lower deck of the Polo Grounds to win the pennant in the greatest comeback in baseball history.

In Josh Prager's book *The Echoing Green*, he writes a very poetic view looking back over those fifty years. Branca had worn the horns of the goat, taken all the guff, the hate mail, and the brunt an endless barbs for throwing that fatal pitch. Ralph, a man of integrity and high morals, never cried, "cheat" or offered any alibi. He suffered the consequences with dignity. While on the other hand, Thomson basked in the wonderful glow of the hero, made lots of appearances and money, but never mentioned the telescope. Prager writes that in the end Thomson was actually the "dodger." He dodged the truth while Branca was truly the "giant" for handling with such great character the demeaning circumstance of being the goat.

When Herman Franks, the Giant coach who manned the telescope and forwarded the signs to the bullpen, died in 2012, I called my teammate Ralph Branca, who also knew Franks. As I told Ralph, old Giants never die . . . they just steal away.

Koufax

I was privileged to play with several Hall of Famers; most of them were position players, not pitchers. In 1955, a young, handsome Jewish left-handed pitcher joined us from the sandlots of Brooklyn. His name was Sandy Koufax.

The Dodgers had a large farm system with some eight hundred players under contract. About two hundred of them were pitchers. However, Koufax could not be one of them because of a bonus he was paid, preventing him from being sent to the minor leagues. This inexperienced 20-year-old was a big leaguer and had never pitched an inning in professional baseball. This proved to be a major disadvantage to Sandy.

In baseball, you never see a first-round draft pick go straight into the lineup of a big league team. You do see it frequently in both the NFL and the NBA. But Sandy, a very intelligent and sensitive young man, seemed bothered that he had leap-frogged some two hundred minor league pitchers and got his Dodger uniform handed to him.

Naturally, he struggled in his few appearances in games. He threw hard but was wild and unpolished. In Sandy's first five years, he had a record of 36 wins and 40 losses.

Sandy's demeanor was quiet, polite, and reserved enough that he never asked for advice. He was expected to learn on the job, and it was a struggle.

In 1959 in the Dodger clubhouse, Sandy confided in me and said he was thinking about quitting baseball, buying into a radio station in Los Angeles. Later that season he told me he had been reconsidering and felt he owed the Dodgers one last try. He said, "I'm going to spring training one more time and [will] give it an all-out try. If after that I still feel this way, I will retire."

Well the seven seasons that followed are history and you could look them up; they include four no-hitters, one a perfect game, with Koufax on the mound. Sandy also boasted a World Series strikeout record of 15 in one game vs the N.Y. Yankees and three seasons of 25 wins or more over that time span. Over his 12-year career, he tallied forty shutouts and 2396 strike outs in 2324 innings and Hall of Fame induction.

Sandy attended the University of Cincinnati out of high school, and was a basketball star there. Imagine, baseball might not have been his best sport.

The Breathless Chicken

Once I became an established player and my job as a pitcher was secure, spring training was a delight. But when you're a young hopeful trying to make a team, spring training can be full of fear, anxiety, and heavy pressure.

Gary Ingram was one of several young outfielders trying to make the cut, and Dodger manager Tommy Lasorda would be the final judge and jury.

It was the end of spring training and the team would be leaving the next day for Los Angeles, but only with the players who made the roster. Gary Ingram was a very personable and well-liked young man. He took a lot of kidding, and at some point he had acquired the nickname "Chicken." Chicken had competed hard for a spot, but so had two or three other out-fielders. Inevitably, there was only room for one on the final roster.

Early on the day of departure, Chicken was summoned to manager Lasorda's office. This was showdown time, and Chicken's nerves were plenty on edge.

When he got to Lasorda's office and went inside, the office was empty. A couple of players lounging outside the door said, "Go on in, he's in there." So Chicken cautiously proceeded. Lasorda called from the lavatory. "I'm in here, come on in." Chicken was dumbfounded to see Lasorda sitting on the throne. "Come on in," he said. "And shut the door." Inside this small cramped space he stood facing Lasorda. Chicken said the air was heavy and the smell was strong. "Well son," said Lasorda. "We've been watching you closely all spring." Chicken said to himself, *Here it comes, the bad news.* "You had a good spring and have a bright future, but you still have to improve in some areas." *I'm headed back to the minors*, thinks Chicken. There was no fan blowing and the air was getting heavier. Lasorda continues, "And so the coaches and I have made a decision. It was a tough one and we all know how much you wanted that final spot, so here is what we have decided. . . . You've made the squad and you'll be leaving later today with the team for Los Angeles".

Chicken said all of a sudden he smelled lilacs, roses, and honeysuckle and he was breathing clean fresh air . . . He's going to Los Angeles . . .

The Plane Truth

The Dodgers have a long history of being first, not only in baseball standings, but in several other categories as well. Of course, they were first to integrate professional baseball in signing Jackie Robinson, who also was the first black Rookie of the Year, MVP, and Hall of Famer. The Dodgers were also first to use lights, along with Cincinnati, for night baseball in the late 1930's.

The Dodgers were first to use numbers on the front of uniforms so players facing the TV camera could be identified. I also saw the first game televised in color at Ebbets Field, Brooklyn.

The Dodgers were the first major league organization to commit to move to the west coast. They were also the first team to use the airplane instead of trains or buses.

Bud Holman, businessman in Vero Beach, was responsible for the Dodgers leasing an abandoned naval air station, which eventually became the famous Dodgertown Spring Training base for sixty years. Holman was also on the board of directors of the Dodgers, along with Walter O'Malley. The directors had decided to purchase an airplane to fly the team to various spring training games around Florida. Holman was also a friend of Eddie Rickenbacker, president of Eastern Air Lines.

One night in Ft. Lauderdale, Florida, Holman and Rickenbacker were engaged in a game of dice. In the hours that followed Holman had a winning streak and had won a big pot. When Rickenbacker finally conceded, Holman said, "I don't want the money. I want an airplane." Rickenbacker gave him the pick of a line of planes. Then Holman gave the plane to the Dodgers.

And so the Dodgers were not only the first team to fly, but also they were the first to fly a DC3 won in a crap game.

Our Choice

This is the tale of one of the most invaluable lessons that I can recall from baseball during my career. It is a lesson from which I still benefit daily.

Branch Rickey was a graduate of Ohio Wesleyan University, as was his close friend Dr. Norman Vincent Peale. Betty and I met Dr. Peale one evening at his church in Manhattan, the Marble Collegiate Church on 5th Ave and 29th Street.

When Dr. Peale was a young college student, a professor kept him after class one day and gave him a royal chewing out. "Norman", he said. "I'm going to flunk you if you don't shake yourself and respond to my questions in class. When called on, you stammer, look at the floor, and never get the answer out."

Well, Dr. Peale with his head down, went outside and sat on the steps reflecting on the dressing down he had just received. Then, in an attitude of despair, he uttered a prayer. "Lord", he said. "You can take a drunk out of the gutter and turn his life around. You can take a life that seems lost and make a new life. Then why can't you cure me of this terrible inferiority complex I have?"

Dr. Peale managed to get through college and seminary and became a powerful preacher and one of the great communicators of his day, both in the spoken and written word. He is the author of the famous best-selling book *The Power of Positive Thinking*, which has sold millions of copies over many years and is still in print.

When he was ninety years old, he was guest speaker on a nationally televised program one Sunday morning. Somewhat feeble and unsteady at the podium, he told the story of his youth and his uncertain future as a pastor. Then he stunned the audience when he said, "You know, I have never lost that awful self-defeating inferiority complex, that's been there all along. However, my faith has kept it from being my master."

The lesson: We can't change who we are, but we can choose who or what is our master.

High Praise

When I grew up in the 1930s, baseball was king of all sports, truly America's pastime. Boys played baseball, ate and slept baseball, and dreamed baseball dreams. We made our own diamonds in vacant lots, cow pastures, and city boys made them in the streets.

When I threw a tennis ball against our old barn door, from the back of the house to a strike zone drawn in chalk, there was always one scenario I was envisioning at the plate—I was always pitching to Babe Ruth in a World Series. I couldn't count how many times I struck out Babe Ruth.

Flash-forward to 1948, and I made the big leagues with the Brooklyn Dodgers and won my first five games. The following year we were in my first World Series. Naturally I had my mother and dad plus Betty's mother and dad in New York for the series. I showed them around the city and after a series game I took them to a famous New York restaurant, Toots Shores. At Toots Shores it was likely you would see a famous movie star or a high-profile celebrity from any walk of life up close and personal.

As we were eating dinner, a gentleman approached our table and in a very polite manner inquired if I was Carl Erskine, of the Dodgers. Much flattered and somewhat embarrassed I confirmed that I was. He said, "A lady at the table behind you would like to speak with you." I rose, turned around, and said hello. The lady said, "I'm Claire Ruth, Mrs. Babe Ruth, and I was told you were here. You came to the Dodgers last year,

1948, and Babe was in the hospital at that time. However, he watched every game on television of the New York teams and he saw you pitch a couple of times. Babe said, 'That Erskine kid is gonna be a good pitcher.' I just thought you would like to know that."

Babe Ruth died in late summer of 1948.

What Are the Odds?

The Dodgers made a good will tour of Japan in 1956. We played there for five weeks in major cities and U.S. military bases. One city was Hiroshima, where the first atomic bomb was dropped. This was only ten years after WWII ended. The Dodger team laid a wreath and had a short ceremony at the monument marking the epicenter of the bomb.

We played the Tokyo Giants and drew big crowds to all our games. The two teams could not speak to each other because of the language barrier, so we sat silent as we flew Japanese Airlines to various cities. On one flight a rumor circulated up and down the aisle on our side, that the Japanese pilot was a former Kamikaze pilot. That created quite a buzz until someone asked why is he still flying, shouldn't he be dead? The answer came from a few rows back, "His nickname is Chicken." I have to admit I cleaned that up a bit.

We flew into a U.S. Army base in Sappora. The ballpark was very small and I was scheduled to pitch. With such short fences and the overflow crowd seated inside the fence on the outfield grass, this had all the earmarks of a high-scoring game. After nine innings, the score was 1 to 0 in favor of the Dodgers. Duke Snider hit a home run, and I faced only 27 batters, the minimum in a nine-inning game. The Giants got one hit, and was erased on a double play. I walked one batter, and he was caught stealing. . . .

Almost sixty years later my grandson Luke married into the Ealum family. His father-in-law Darrel was contacted by a cousin, James Brock, Staff Sergeant, stationed at Sappora, and had been at the game in 1956. He took this picture of me leaving the ball park.

A Blue Blood

One of the most popular personalities in all of sports is Tommy Lasorda. Tommy and I were minor league pitchers in the Dodgers large system of 26 minor league teams. He was left-handed, I was right-handed. Tommy was a bulldog. He asked no quarter and certainly never gave one. If you weren't a Dodger, you were the enemy. Tommy truly loved baseball and was forever loyal to the Dodgers. There has never been a better diplomat for baseball than he, and there has never been a name more synonymous with Dodgers than Tommy. He often says, "If you go to church and say your prayers, when you die you'll go to Dodgertown."

Tommy has asked to have a special tombstone. His wish is to have a stone with a special place for a current Dodgers schedule, so when people come to visit the graves of their loved ones, they'll say, "Let's go over to Tommy's grave and see if the Dodgers are playing today."

Tommy met his wife Jo when he played in the minors. She has been at his side through every level of baseball and watched him play or manage in: the low minors, winter leagues, the Olympics, and World Series. She was there when he was inducted into Baseball's Hall of Fame, as a manager. She has been a personal witness to his devotion to baseball.

One day Jo says to Tommy, "Let's face it Tommy, you love baseball more than you love me."

"Oh come on," said Tommy. "I love you more than basketball, football, tennis, hockey, wrestling . . ." Tommy bleeds Dodger Blue.

Blood Money

I have always had a good relationship with baseball fans. That's because I do respect the part fans play in keeping the game alive, and in fact, in keeping old timers like me alive.

I get an average of ten to twelve fan letters each day. These letters come from all over, even from Japan, Latin America, Israel, Germany, and Canada. Because I answer my mail, I tend to get more mail. Many times a fan will alert me to a personal stat I never knew existed. For instance, I had a personal goal of getting a thousand strike outs in the big leagues. When I retired I was nineteen short. I was always disappointed. Years after my retirement I received a fan letter from a 12-year-old boy from Kansas. He said, "Mr. Erskine, you had a fine career and counting the 31 strike outs you got in World Series games, you got over 1,000." See why I like fans.

My home town of Anderson, Indiana is full of people who have followed my career and given great support. Even to this day I feel surrounded by great fans. One of them is Eddie Ray, a local contractor and collector of baseball memorabilia, many in his collection are my baseball cards. Over the years we have become good friends.

When I retired from baseball in 1960, I became a bank officer in our local First National Bank. Eddie came into our loan department and applied for a $6,000 loan to buy a tractor. Our loan officers couldn't qualify him, so he was turned down. Eddie came to my office, "Carl, you know me. You know I'm good for that loan, now just pick up that phone and call those guys, tell them to make me that loan, you can do it. I need that tractor." "I won't override my loan officers but we will take a new look at it." "No, no, all you have to do is tell those guys and they will do it." I tried all the diplomacy I could muster but Eddie was not deterred. Finally he moved his chair closer to my desk, leaned forward toward me, looked straight into my eyes and asked, "Do you remember when you had your big hip surgery?"

"Well yes" I said.

"I gave a pint of blood for you."

I was stunned. It was true. Eddie had gone to the hospital and donated blood for me. Yes, he got the loan and yes he paid it back. In sales the pivotal moment is "the close." You can't beat that one.

Buzzed

Some of the smoothest plays in baseball are not on the field but across the desk of the owner or General Manager of the team during salary negotiations. Before free agency in the 1970s, players were their own agents. It was an unfair fight. The player's contract had a clause called "The Reserve Clause." When a player signed a contract with a team, he was the property of that team forever. The team could sell, trade, or lease the player at any time, but the player was bound to that team and could not negotiate with any other team. Yet another subtle clause in the fine print, the team was only obligated to pay the player 30 days of his contract if he was released. So the player had both hands tied behind his back. Actually the only negotiation was that the player was happy playing for the next season. The contracts were always for just one year.

There are literally hundreds of stories about players trying to get a raise after a good season. The minimum salary in the majors at that time was $5,000. In 1951, pitcher Ned Garver of the St. Louis Browns won 20 games for the last place team; he had 24 complete games and he also hit .305. Owner Bill Veeck said, "No raise Ned, we could have finished last without you." When Branch Rickey signed young Tommy Lasorda to a meager minor league contract, he asked Tommy not to tell anyone what his salary was. Tommy said, "You don't have to worry Mr. Rickery about me telling anyone what I'm making, I'm just as ashamed of it as you are." After I won twenty games in 1953, I expected a nice raise. I had to settle for getting my teeth fixed.

One classic story is about quiet, soft spoken giant of a man Gil Hodges, Dodgers first baseman, when he negotiated his contract with General Manager Buzzie Bavasi. Gil asked for $24,000. Buzzie countered with $20,000. The discussion lasted several minutes, then silence. Finally Buzzie said, "Okay Gil, let's do this a fair way. I'll take three slips of paper, on one I'll write $24,000, on another I'll write $20,000, and on the third slip, a figure in the middle of $22,000. You can draw a slip and I'll pay you what you draw." Gil agreed, so Buzzie wrote the figures, folded each piece tightly, shook them up and presented them to Gil in his cupped hands. Gil drew, opened the slip, $20,000. Years later Buzzie admitted he had this number on all three slips.

The Rest of the Story

The *New York* writers voted "The Shot Heard Round the World," as the greatest sports event of the last century. Yes, the Bobby Thomson walk-off, three-run-homer beat the 1951 Brooklyn Dodgers to win the National League pennant, after the Dodgers had held a 13.5 game lead in late August.

Bobby Thomson was the great hero hitting a fastball thrown by pitcher Ralph Branca into the left field stands at the Polo Grounds. Branca, my teammate and an outstanding young pitcher who had won 21 games when he was just 21 years old, was devastated. He got boos; hate mail and the humiliation associated with failure under pressure. I was there and experienced the aftermath in our locker room. I can still see Ralph, completely spent, sprawled a crossed the steps leading up to the trainer's room, and the big number 13 on his back. Ralph would carry the losers load for the next fifty years.

Josh Prager, a writer for the *Wall Street Journal*, had heard rumors about the fantastic finish of the New York Giants in 1951, possibly being tainted by a cheating scheme. Prager decided to do some intensive "investigative" reporting into the rumors.

Josh made contact with a third string catcher from the 1951 Giants, Sal Evars, who was still around. In his interview with Evars, the truth came out. Yes, the Giants, while under manager Leo Durocher, had rigged a system using a telescope stationed in the centerfield window of the Giants's clubhouse, with a wire and buzzer to the Giants bullpen in right center field. Herman Franks, a former catcher was Leo's bench coach. Leo assigned Franks to man the telescope, because, as an experienced catcher, he could easily understand the opponent catchers' signs, and relay them to the bullpen. One buzz meant fastball, two a curve or slider. Setting in the bullpen, Evars would hold a white towel on his lap. He would remain still on fast ball and raise the towel on curve. From the batter's box you could look straight at the pitcher and easily see the Giants bullpen and Evars.

And so, Josh Prager writes the rest of the story and in doing so finishes with a classic description of both the hero Thompson and the goat Branca. In his book *Echoing Green* he writes, [paraphrased] "In the end it was Thompson who was the 'dodger.' He dodged the truth. He took the sign but never mentioned the telescope. He just lived the life of a hero. While Branca was really the 'giant' because he never cried 'cheat,' although it was suspected. Branca never alibied. He suffered the indignities with class."

In 2014 Herman Franks, the man behind the telescope passed away. I contacted my friend and teammate Ralph Branca, and simply said. "Old Giants never die, they just steal away."

The Same Game

Baseball has prided itself on its unchanging format for over a century. It's true, the baselines are still 90 feet and it's still three strikes and three outs per inning. Other sports have made many changes, often to produce more scoring. I'm just glad baseball didn't count two runs for upper deck home runs, as basketball scores three points for a longer basket.

In spite of baseballs contention of few changes, there indeed have been several. The most obvious is the American League's "designated hitter." Baseball owners and Commissioner have always "tweaked" the game to try and give fans what they want, more offence. When pitching becomes too dominant, the mound has been slightly lowered or the top of the strike zone lowered.

At one time the top of the strike zone was the arm pits. Today it is at the belt, a lowering of 9 to 10 inches, eliminating the high strike, which is hardest to hit. Batting gloves, helmets, shin guards all favor the hitter. Do I sound like a pitcher?

Major League baseballs have been manufactured by Rawlings for decades. The company always stands by the contention that the same materials have been used over the years. However, in my seasons of 1948 to 1960, the balls were hand stitched. The ball was softer and stitches higher. Today the balls are machine stitched, making them tighter and more lively.

Ever wonder why major league bats explode, shattering into pieces? In past decades a bat would crack and usually could be fixed with small tacks and tape. Bat speed represents power. The lighter the bat, means the more speed the bat has. According to Hillerich & Bradsby, makers of the Louisville Slugger bats, the signature bat of the major leagues, players want lighter bats but same larger barrel and length. To accomplish this, the ash billet's of which a bat is lathe turned, is kiln dried to take out more moisture. That takes the "guts" out of the bat, so when a 90-mile-an-hour fast ball is mishit (not on the sweet spot) it explodes and pieces fly everywhere.

Another change is the domed stadiums, where wind and sun problems are eliminated and artificial turf assures no bad hops, muddy fields, or rained-out games.

The one thing that has not changed, and sets baseball apart from other sports is no clock. In a nine inning game, the winning team must record 27 outs, no matter that it might take all night. Sometimes it does.

Tense

Gene Hermanski, Dodgers outfielder, fit the role perfectly as one of the zany characters who played at Ebbets Field in Brooklyn. Gene had an infectious laugh and sense of humor that kept our team loose. He's the one who took the tension out of a trying situation in Atlanta when we played a preseason game there in 1949. The Klu Klux Klan had picketed our bus because we had a black player on our team name Jackie Robinson. A letter was delivered to our manager Burt Shotton in the clubhouse. The letter read: "If Jackie Robinson takes the field today he will be shot." Believe me this young team was very quiet in that sobering moment. Hermanski from the back of the room: "Hey Skipper, if we all wore number 42 they won't know who to shoot at." The room exploded with laughter; the tension was gone. Jackie played that day and no shots were fired.

Peewee Reese, our team captain, added to the fun on the field. While warming up next to Jackie along the sideline, Peewee yelled at Jackie, "Hey buddy, do you mind moving over a bit? This guy might be a bad shot."

Down Under

Dodgers outfielder Gene Hermanski was an avid golfer. He had all the latest equipment and dressed like a touring professional. However he never broke 100 on his score card.

Gene was a power hitter in baseball. He could hit a ball out of sight. Same for his golf shots, but he was never deterred. After a round Gene was asked, "How'd you do today?"

"Well," he replied in a loud voice, "I had a seven on number one and eight on two, a seven on three, and then dammit I blew up."

I was player representative and had roomed with Gene. He had helped me win my first start in the big leagues by hitting three home runs in that game. He came to me one day and said, "Carl, there's something I want you to do for me. When I die I want to be buried on the golf course. Now here is how I want it done. I want to be buried between the ninth green and the tenth tee. Here's what I want on my marker: HERE LIES GENE HERMANSKI, SIX UNDER AT THE TURN."

Twice as Nice

Every baseball player dreams of being in a World Series. I was privileged to be on Dodgers teams that played in six. I personally got to pitch in eleven games, which is tenth on the all-time list of appearances by a pitcher. It's a fantasy to ever expect to hold any kind of World Series record. I did have one for strike outs, fourteen, but no more. Sandy Koufax broke it with fifteen. However there is a category in which I do have a World Series record at the time of this writing.

In the 1953 World Series, I faced the powerful New York Yankees. Hitting third in the lineup was catcher Yogi Berra, a strong left-handed hitter. On orders from my manager Charlie Dressen, I was to throw a knockdown pitch to Berra and loosen him up from his dug in batting stance. My first try hit Yogi in the ribs. Told to do it right the next time, now my fast ball hit Yogi on the right elbow. **World Series Record.** It's the first and only time in World Series' history (112 World Series through 2016) that the same pitcher hit the same batter twice in the same game. You can look it up.

Making Do

Tommy Lasorda has been in baseball for nearly 70 years. He has a passion for baseball and truly has given his life for the game.

Tommy has many pitching records in the AAA International League. Injuries kept him from making it to the majors; but he has stayed in the game in any capacity, done all the dirty jobs just to keep in touch. He has spent many years managing in the minors, riding old busses, staying in fleabag hotels, and working for little pay. Finally he emerged as a Hall of Fame manager and baseball immortal. However he never forgot where he came from.

Once, when in a low minors, a player came to Tommy, his manager and asked if he could use the whirlpool because he had hurt his ankle. In a surprised voice Tommy said, "Whirlpool, are you kidding?"

"Oh wait, yes we do have a whirlpool. Go in the crapper, stick your foot in the pot and flush."

"Who was the toughest hitter you faced?"
The answer:

Stan the Man

S tan the Man" was the name given to Cardinals Stan Musial by the rabid Brooklyn Dodgers fans, because he hit so well at Ebbets Field. In fact our Dodgers players were very irritated at our fans for cheering Musial when he came to bat. He was the enemy.

Stan was a lifetime .330 hitter (exactly what he hit against me). He also hit over 400 home runs and led the National League seven times in hitting average. Yet he was a humble spirit and well respected throughout baseball and beyond. I remember when he hit his 400th home run, he remarked, "Not bad for a singles hitter." The nation mourned when he died a few years ago.

I received a call from a fan who really knew his baseball stats. He asked me if I knew who I faced the most times in my twelve seasons. Of course I did not. He said, "Musial, 164 times." My quick thought, *Why did I pick him?*

Stan and I attended a big baseball bash in Louisville after our playing days. At a private dinner party, Al Hirt, the famous trumpet player, was providing the music. After dinner with Stan and his wife Lil, Stan pulled a harmonica from his coat pocket. "What are you going to do with that," I asked. "I'm going to play a song with Al Hirt." he said.

Jokingly I said, "I wish I had brought my harmonica."

Stan reached back in his pocket and handed me another harmonica. Together we played, "Oh Them Golden Slippers" with Al Hirt. As we returned to our table I said, "Stan, it's a lot easier playing with you than against you."

A Final Thought

As I mentioned in the story titled "The Presidents," I have always held that the greatest quote ever uttered by a major league player was by Babe Ruth in 1930.

But now that quote has fallen to second place behind one that I can relate to—and I bet countless of other players and genuine baseball fans can as well. In his book *Ball Four*, Jim Bouton writes, "I've been gripping a baseball most of my life, only to find out it's the other way around."

Answers: steal home, fielder's choice, and squeeze play.